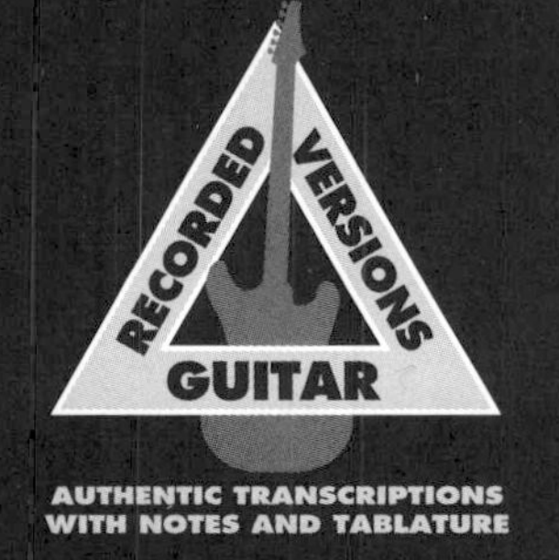

The Avett Brothers

GUITAR COLLECTION

Photo courtesy of The Avett Brothers

Music transcriptions by Pete Billmann, Martin Shellard and David Stocker

ISBN 978-1-4803-6071-6

7777 W. BLUEMOUND RD P.O. BOX 13819 MILWAUKEE, WI 53213

In Australia Contact:
Hal Leonard Australia Pty. Ltd.
4 Lentara Court
Cheltenham, Victoria, 3192 Australia
Email: ausadmin@halleonard.com.au

Visit Hal Leonard Online at
www.halleonard.com

from *Magpie and the Dandelion*

Another Is Waiting

Words and Music by Scott Avett, Timothy Avett and Robert Crawford

Gtr. 1 tuning:
(low to high) E-A-D-G-B-D

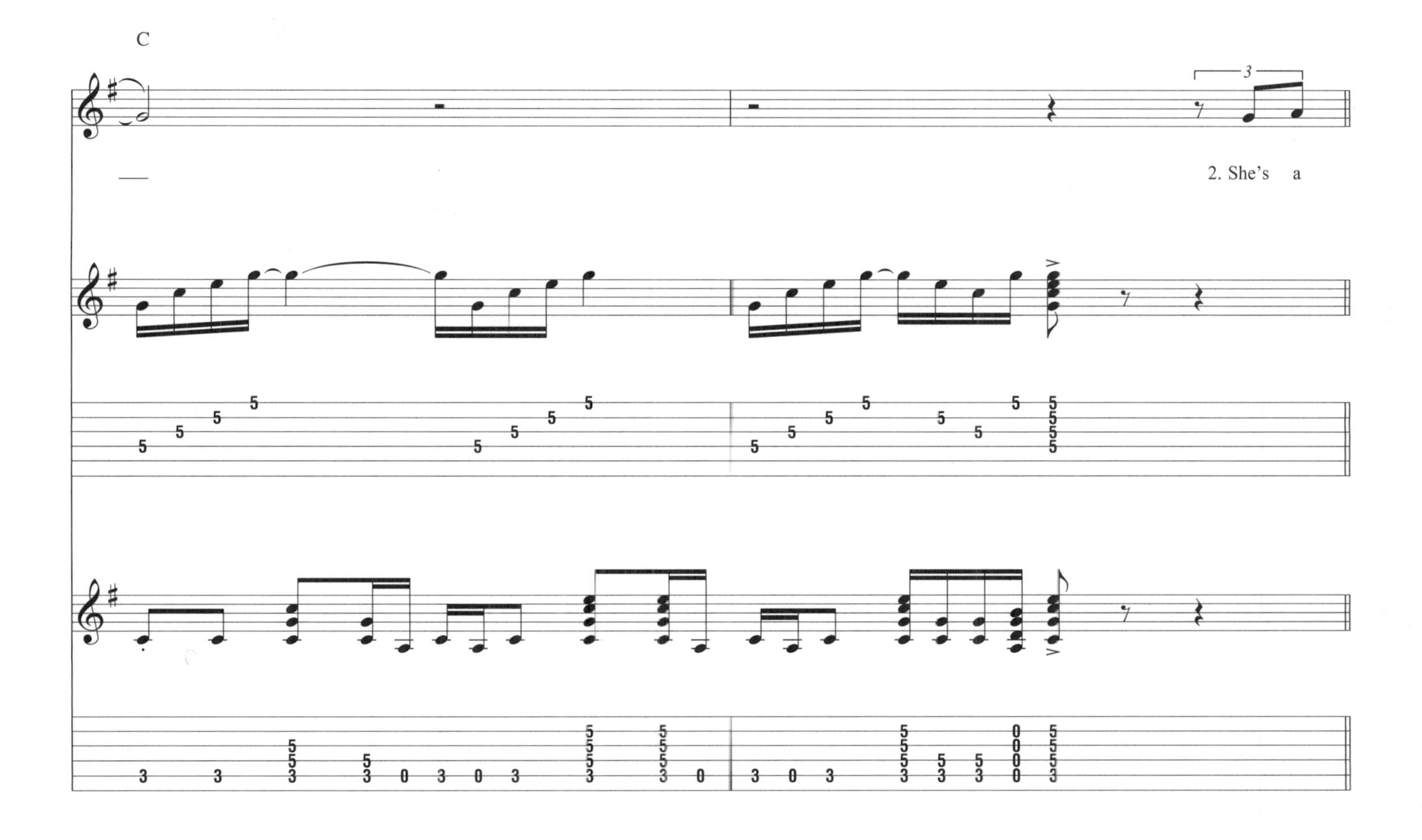
C
2. She's a

Verse
G
Em
Bm
D
rose, she's a queen. But she's star - ing at a mag - a - zine in the dark.

G
Em
Bm
D
On that path, where they doc - tor ev - 'ry pho - to - graph.

Chorus

C
G
C
G
A7
An - oth - er is wait - ing,
she is - n't say - ing an - y -
(She is - n't say - ing an - y -

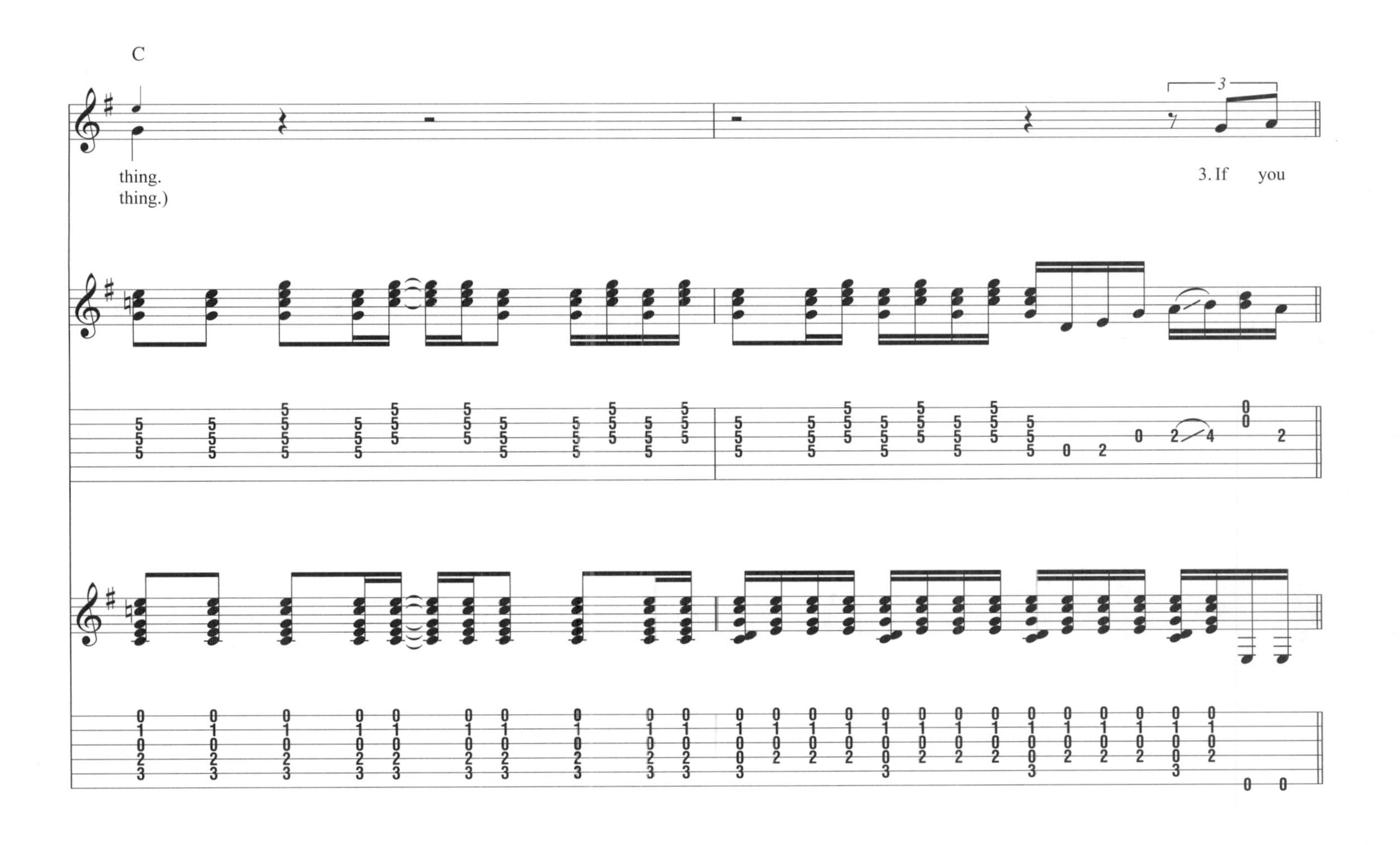
C
thing.
thing.)
3. If you

Verse

G
Em
Bm
D
care, if you like, well, I'm stand - ing in the lan - tern light. With our
let ring
let ring
let ring
let ring

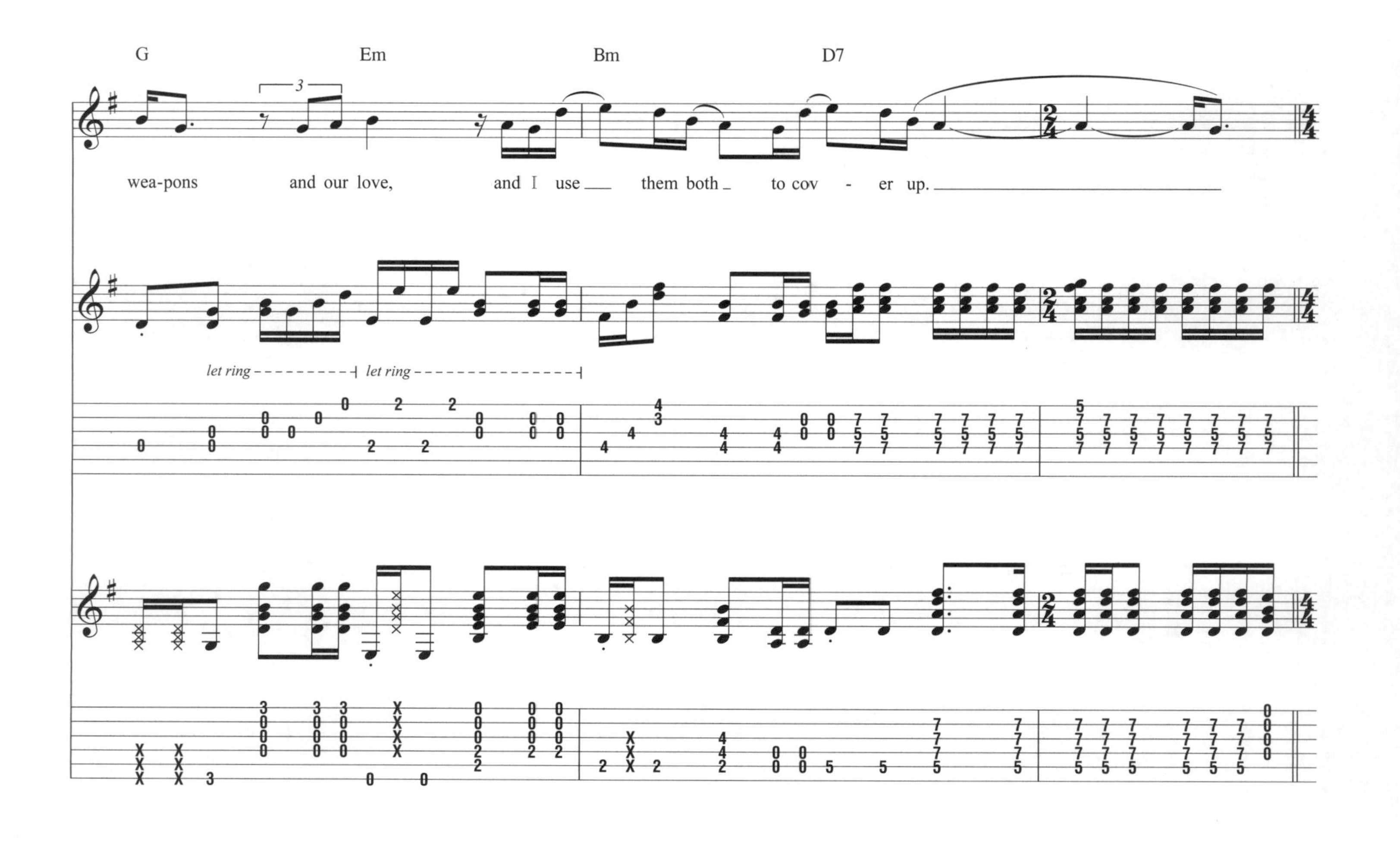
G
Em
Bm
D7
wea-pons and our love, and I use them both to cov - er up.
let ring
let ring

Chorus

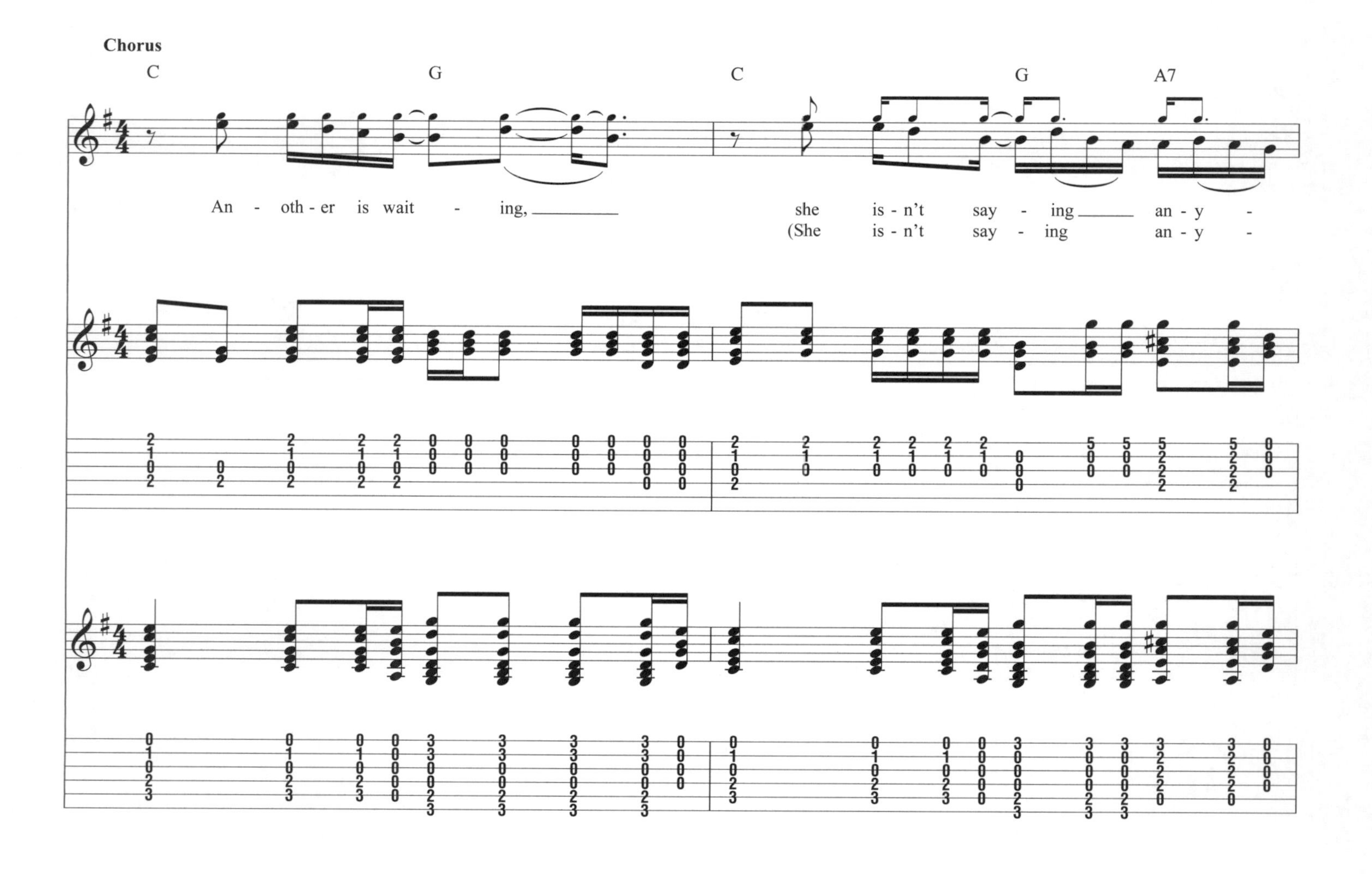
C
G
C
G
A7
An - oth - er is wait - ing, she is - n't say - ing an - y -
(She is - n't say - ing an - y -

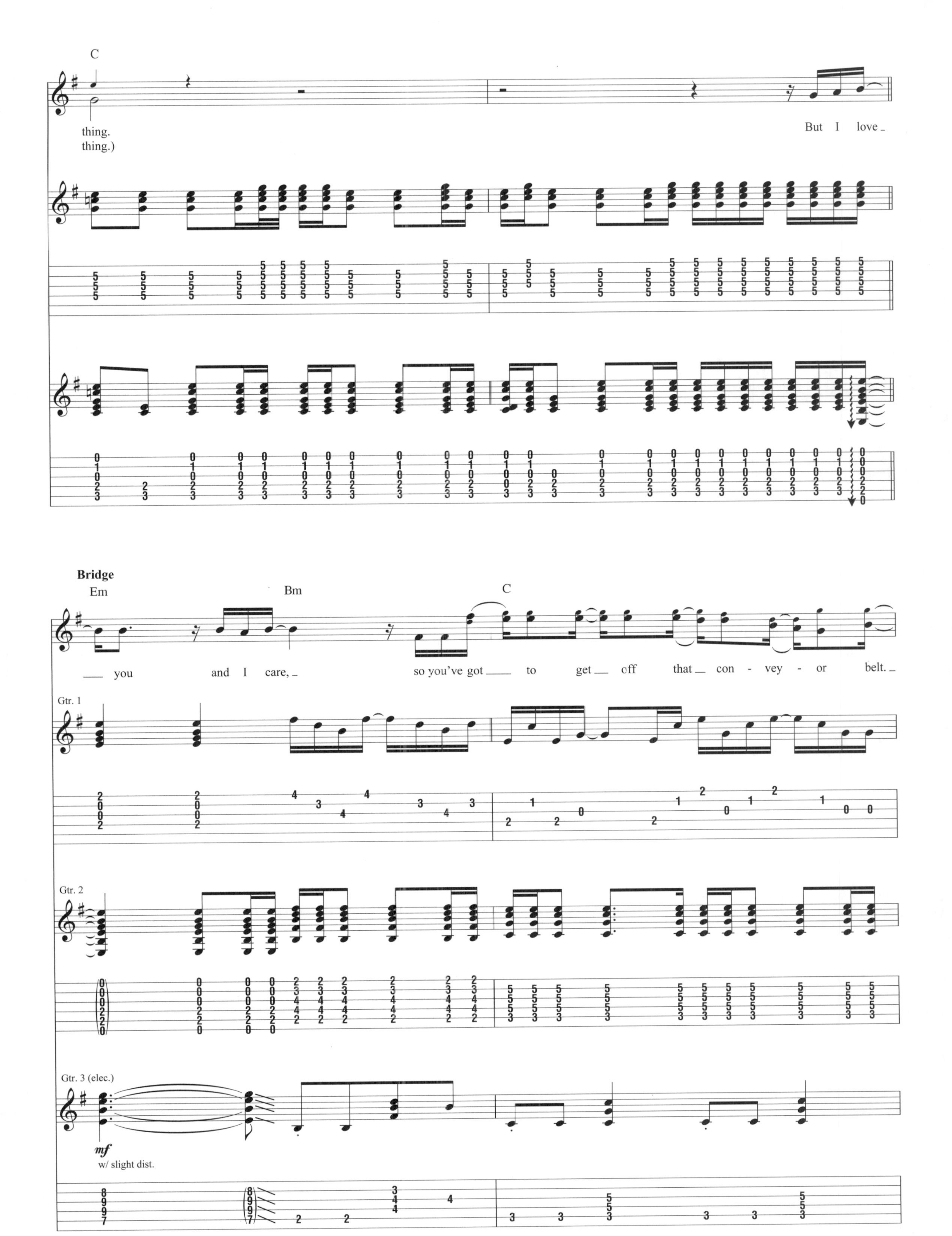
C
thing.
thing.)
But I love
Bridge
Em
Bm
C
you and I care,
so you've got to get off that con - vey - or belt.
Gtr. 1
Gtr. 2
Gtr. 3 (elec.)
mf
w/ slight dist.

Em
Bm
C
If I could, I would come right in and take you off my - self.
D7
4. It's a
Gtr. 1
Gtr. 2
Gtr. 4 (acous.)
mf
Gtr. 3

Verse
G
Em
Gtr. 4 tacet
Bm
D
fake, it's a con, the na - ture of the road you're on, let me
mp
G
Em
Bm
D7
see your skel-e-ton, well be-fore your life is done.
Gtr. 1
Gtr. 2
Gtr. 3

Chorus
C
G
C
G
A7
An - oth - er is wait - ing,
She is - n't say - ing an - y -
(She is - n't say - ing an - y -
mf
C
D
C
G
thing.
thing.)
An - oth - er is wait - ing

C
G
A7
C
She is - n't say - ing any - y - thing.
(She is - n't say - ing an - y - thing.)
G
Harm.

from *The Second Gleam*

Bella Donna

Words and Music by Scott Avett and Timothy Avett

Capo II

*Symbols in parentheses represent chord names respective to capoed guitar. Symbols above represent actual sounding chords.

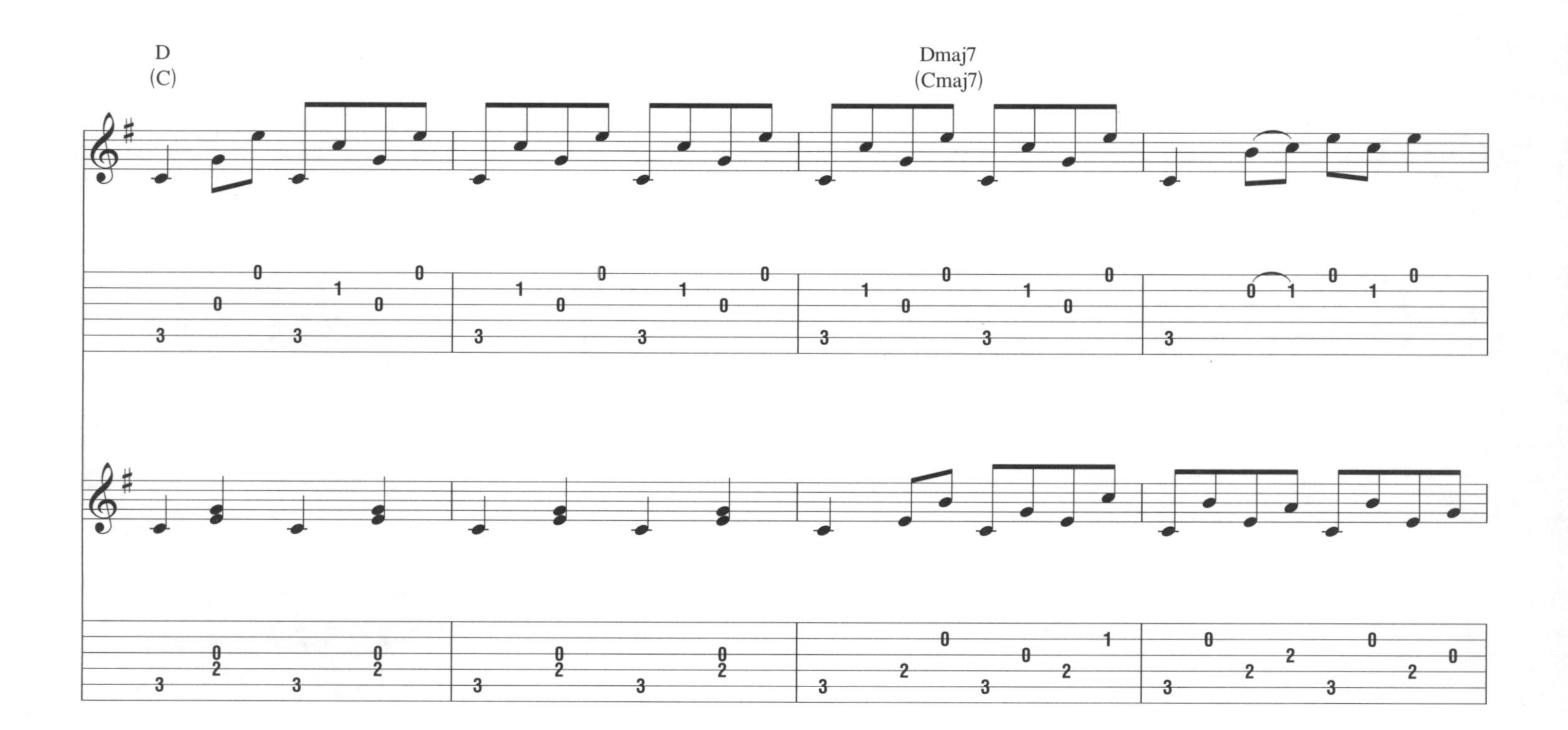

A
(G)
Dmaj7
(Cmaj7)
1. Ba -
Verse
A
(G)
- by, I asked you not to keep me wait -

D
(C)
Dmaj7
(Cmaj7)
- ing.
I told you not to keep me wait -

A
(G)
- ing.
Now the af - ter - noon is fad -

D
(C)
Dmaj7
(Cmaj7)
- ing on.
Interlude
A
(G)
D
(C)
Dmaj7
(Cmaj7)

A
(G)
Dmaj7
(Cmaj7)
2. Don -
Verse
A
(G)
- na,
Bel - la Don - na, have you seen

D
(C)
Dmaj7
(Cmaj7)
me?
And have you ev - er real - ly seen

A
(G)
me
like I want for you to see

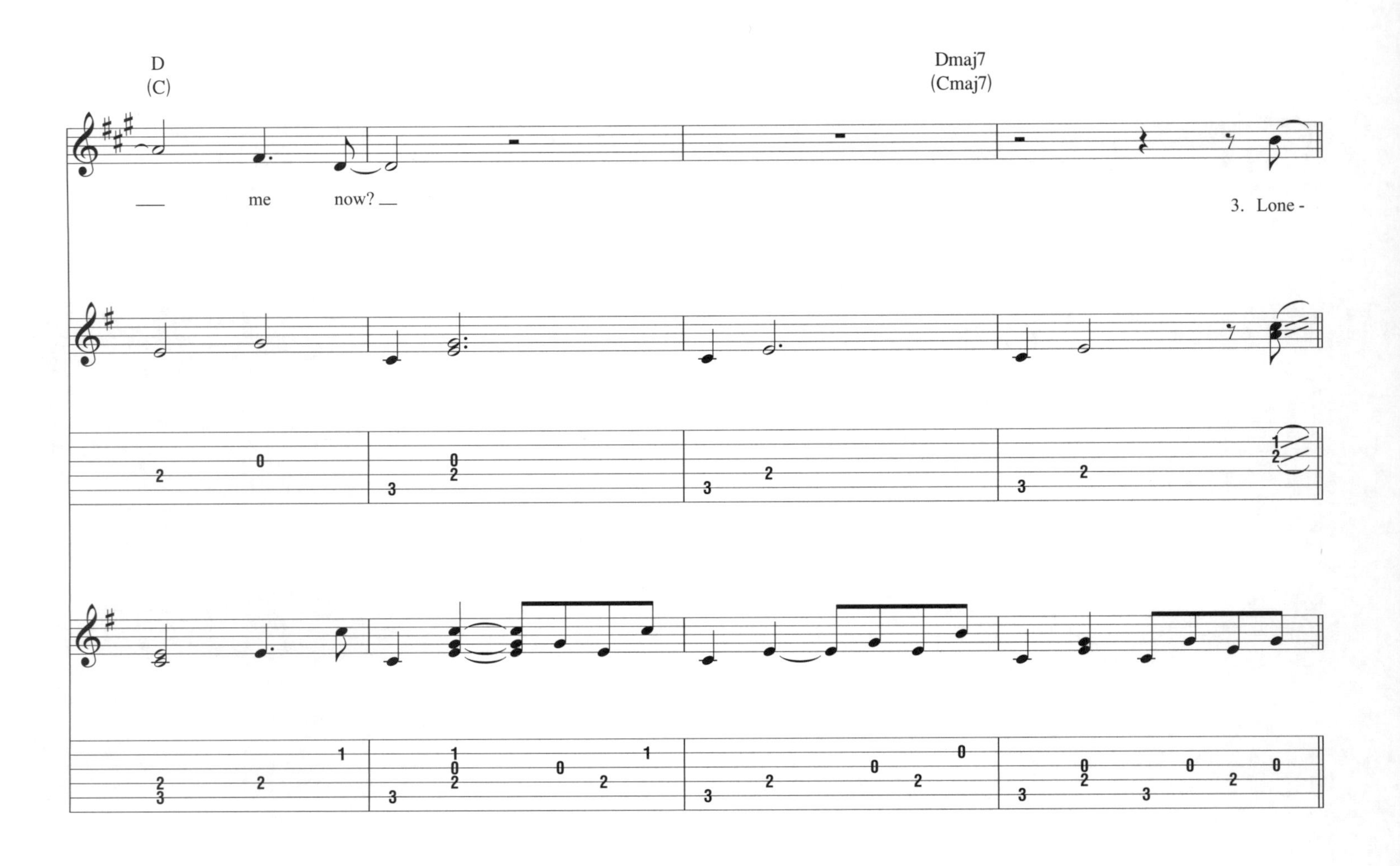
D
(C)
Dmaj7
(Cmaj7)
me now?
3. Lone -

Verse
A
(G)
some,
like you were when you were six -

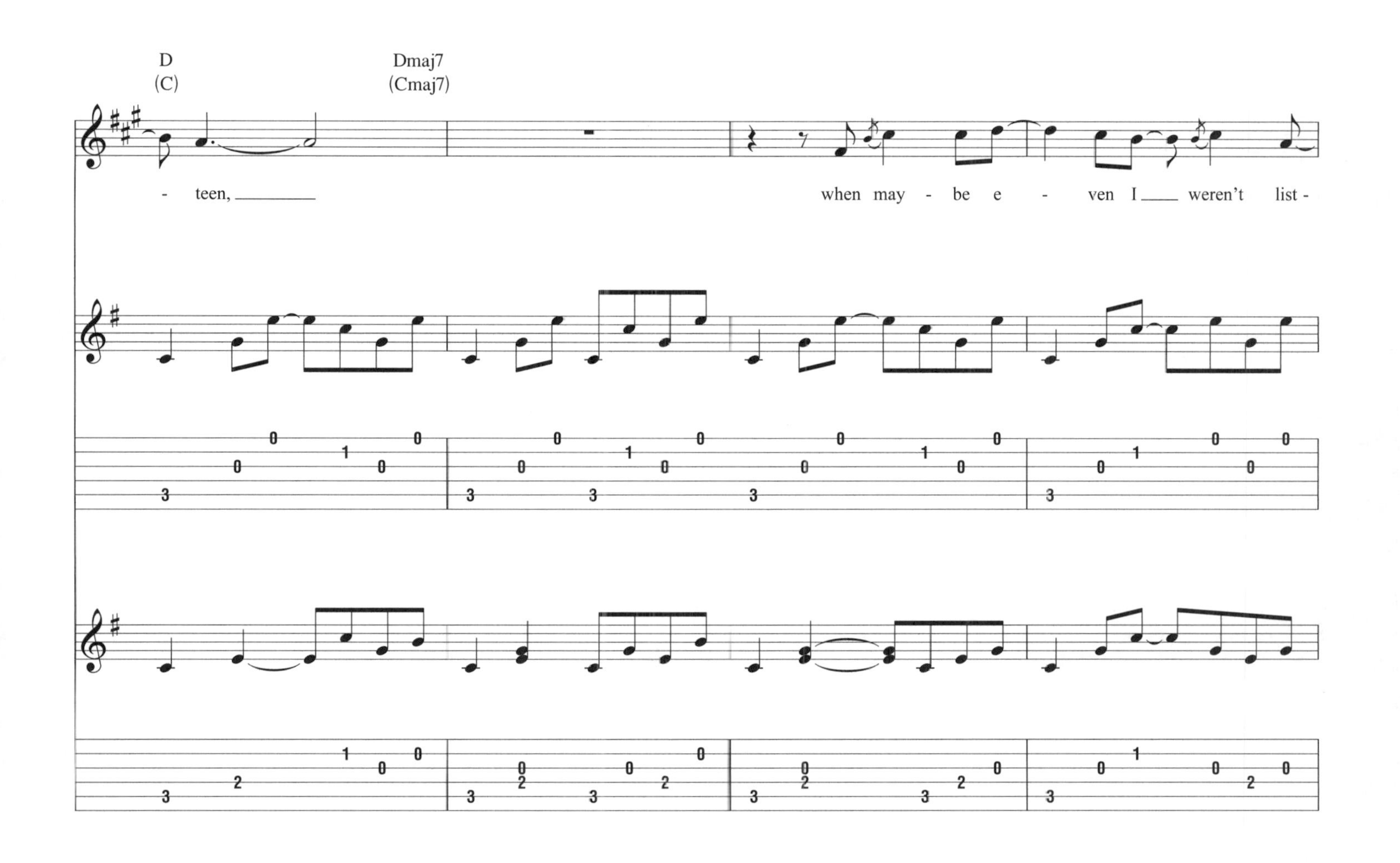
D
(C)
Dmaj7
(Cmaj7)
- teen,
when may - be e - ven I weren't list -

A
(G)
- 'ning.
Did I help when I was

D
(C)
Dmaj7
(Cmaj7)
kiss - ing you?
Interlude
A
(G)
D
(C)
Dmaj7
(Cmaj7)

A
(G)
Dmaj7
(Cmaj7)
4. Don -
Outro-Verse
A
(G)
- na,
Bel - la Don - na, are you list -

D
(C)
Dmaj7
(Cmaj7)
A
(G)
- 'ning?
But were you ev - er real - ly list - 'ning

D
(C)
rit.
like I want for you to lis - ten now?
rit.
rit.

from *Emotionalism*

Die Die Die

Words and Music by Scott Avett, Timothy Avett and Robert Crawford

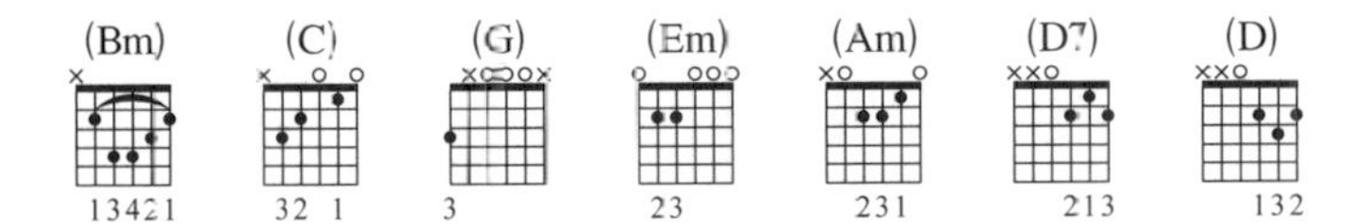

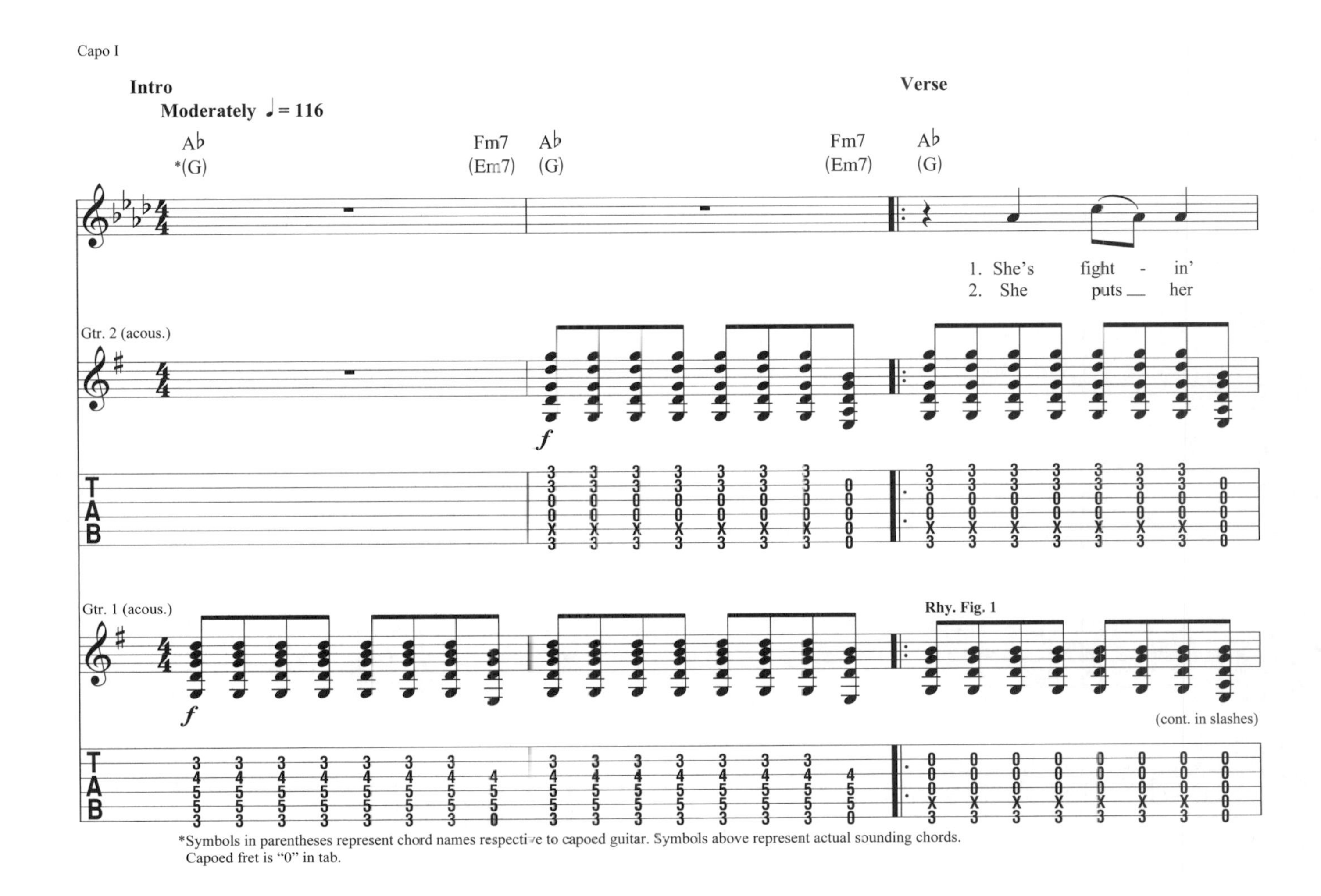

*Symbols in parentheses represent chord names respective to capoed guitar. Symbols above represent actual sounding chords. Capoed fret is "0" in tab.

**See top of page for chord diagrams pertaining to rhythm slashes.

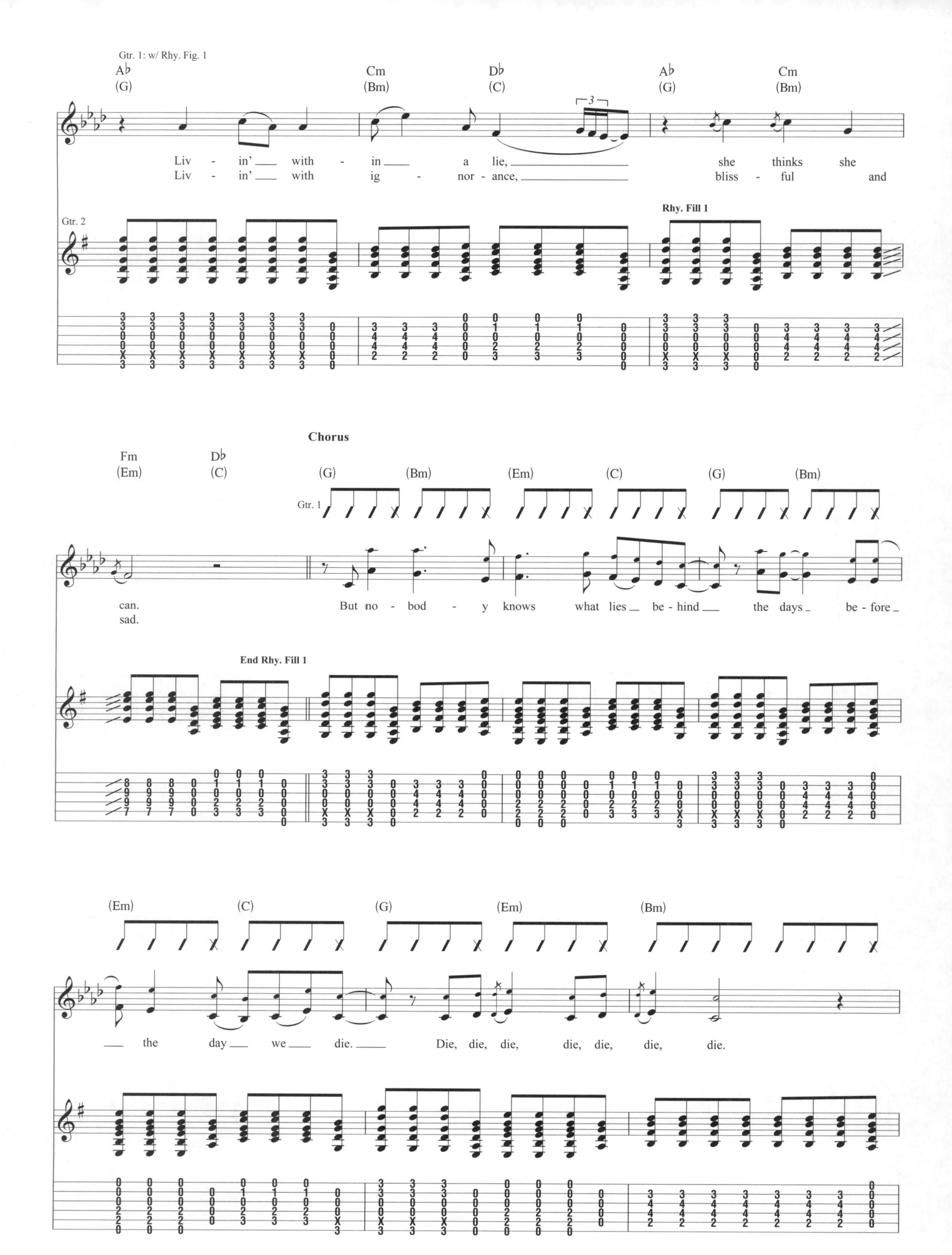
Gtr. 1: w/ Rhy. Fig. 1
A♭ (G) Cm (Bm) D♭ (C) A♭ (G) Cm (Bm)
Liv - in' with - in a lie, she thinks she
Liv - in' with ig - nor - ance, bliss - ful and
Gtr. 2
Rhy. Fill 1
Chorus
Fm (Em) D♭ (C) (G) (Bm) (Em) (C) (G) (Bm)
Gtr. 1
can. But no - bod - y knows what lies be - hind the days be - fore
sad.
End Rhy. Fill 1
(Em) (C) (G) (Em) (Bm)
the day we die. Die, die, die, die, die, die, die.

(G) (Em) (Bm) (C)
Die, die, die, die, die, die, die, die, die, die.
Bridge
(G) (Em) (Am) (D7) (G) (Em)
Rhy. Fig. 2
You can try to swim the sea, but say good - bye to
(Am) (D7) D♭ (C) N.C.
End Rhy. Fig. 2
you and me.
End Rhy. Fig. 2A
(cont. in slashes)

Interlude
(Bm)
(Am)
(Bm)
(Am)
*Gtrs. 1 & 2
(Do, do, do, do, do, do, do, do, do. Do, do, do, do, do, do.
Gtr. 3 (acous.)
f
Gtr. 4 (elec.)
f
w/ clean tone & reverb
*Composite arrangement
(Em)
(Bm)
(C)
Gtrs. 3 & 4 tacet
(D)
Do, do, do, do, do, do, do, do, do.
Do, do.)
let ring
let ring
Bridge
Gtrs. 1 & 2: w/ Rhy. Figs. 2 & 2A (2 times)
A♭
(G)
Fm
(Em)
B♭m
(Am)
E♭7
(D7)
A♭
(G)
Fm
(Em)
B♭m
(Am)
E♭7
(D7)
You can try to swim the sea, you can try to hold the breeze.

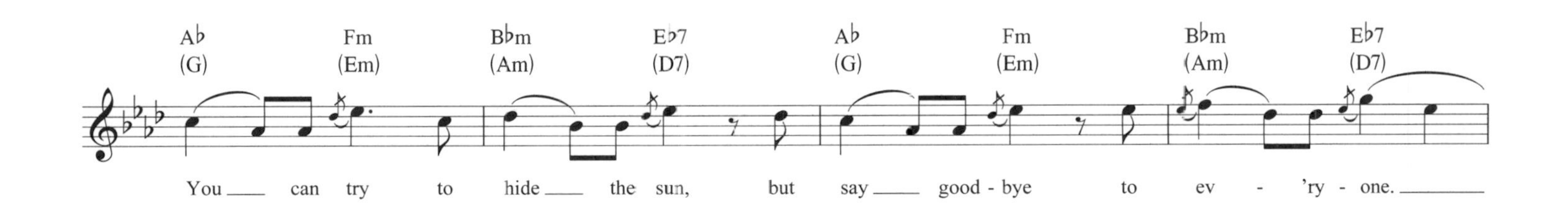
A♭ (G)
Fm (Em)
B♭m (Am)
E♭7 (D7)
You can try to hide the sun, but say good - bye to ev - 'ry - one.

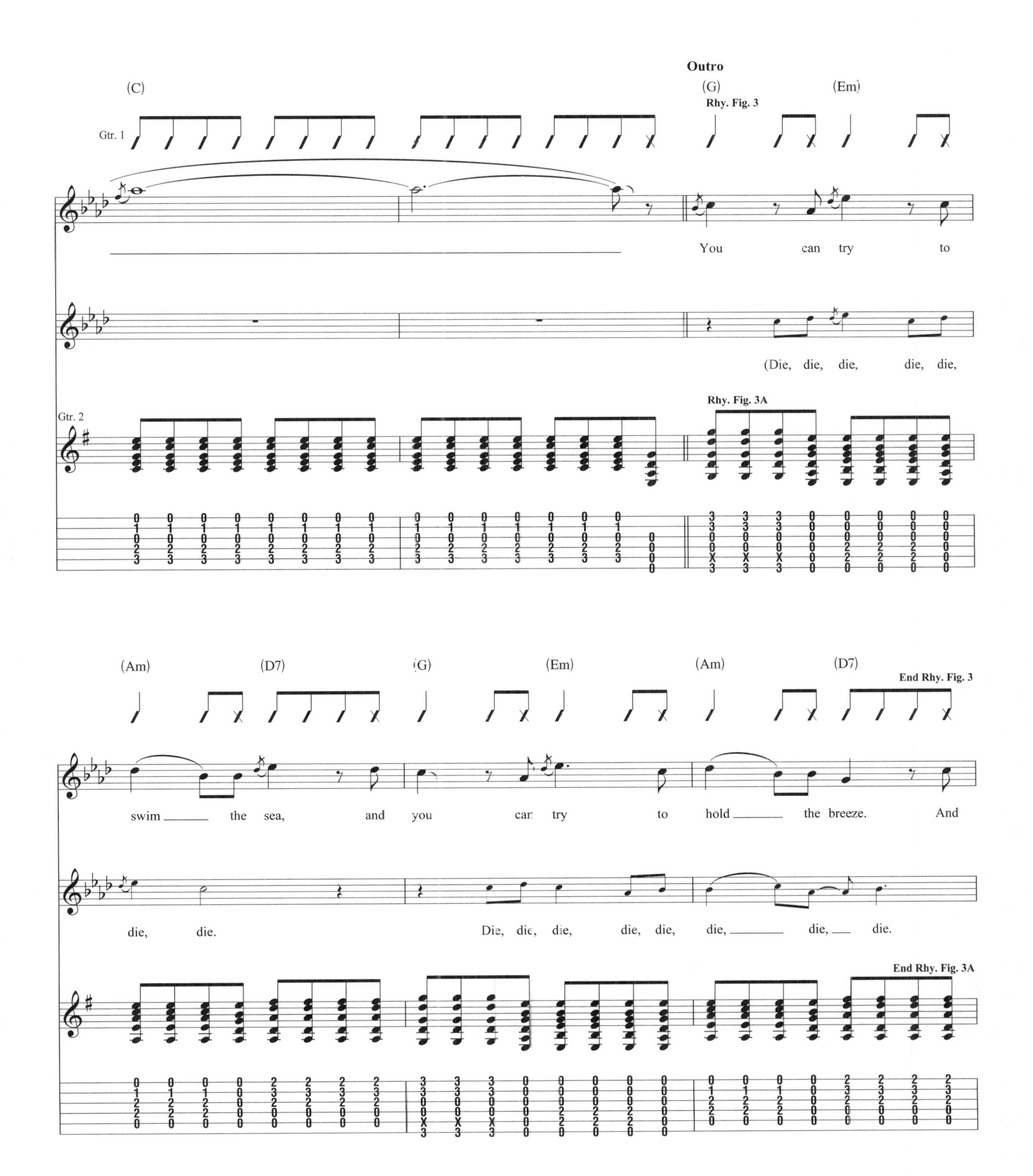
(C)
Outro
(G)
(Em)
Rhy. Fig. 3
Gtr. 1
You can try to
(Die, die, die, die, die,
Rhy. Fig. 3A
Gtr. 2
(Am)
(D7)
End Rhy. Fig. 3
swim the sea, and you can try to hold the breeze. And
die, die. Die, die, die, die, die, die, die, die.
End Rhy. Fig. 3A

Gtrs. 1 & 2: w/ Rhy. Figs. 3 & 3A (3 times)
A♭ (G) Fm (Em) B♭m (Am) E♭7 (D7) A♭ (G) Fm (Em) B♭m (Am) E♭7 (D7)
you can try to hide the sun, but say good - bye to ev - 'ry - one. And
Die, die, die, die, die, die, die.
Die, die, die, die, die, die, die, die.
A♭ (G) Fm (Em) B♭m (Am) E♭7 (D7) A♭ (G) Fm (Em) B♭m (Am) E♭7 (D7)
you can try to swim the sea, and you can try to hold the breeze.
(Die, die, die, die. Die, die, die, die, die, die. Die,
No - bod - y knows what lies be - hind the days be - fore the day we die.
A♭ (G) B♭m (Am) D♭ (C) E♭7 (D7) A♭ (G) Fm (Em) B♭m (Am) E♭7 (D7)
You can try through skin and bone, but you would end up all a - lone.
die, die, die, die. Die, die, die, die, die, die.)
Die, die, die, die, die, die, die.
Die, die, die, die, die, die, die, die.)
(C) (G)
Gtr. 1
Gtr. 2

from *The Carpenter*

February Seven

Words and Music by Scott Avett, Seth Avett and Robert Crawford

Capo IV

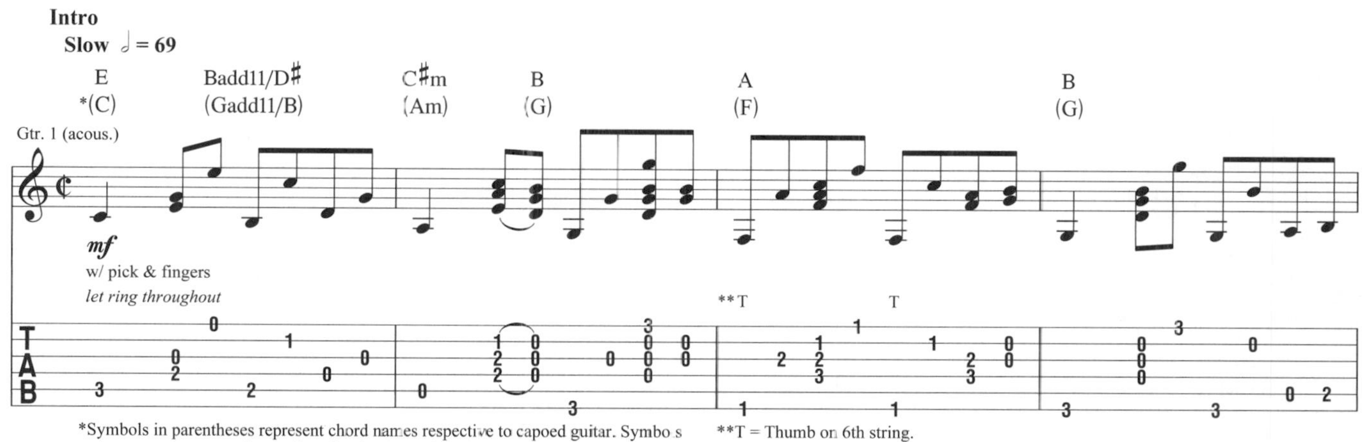

*Symbols in parentheses represent chord names respective to capoed guitar. Symbols above represent actual sounding chords. Capoed fret is "0" in tab.

**T = Thumb on 6th string.

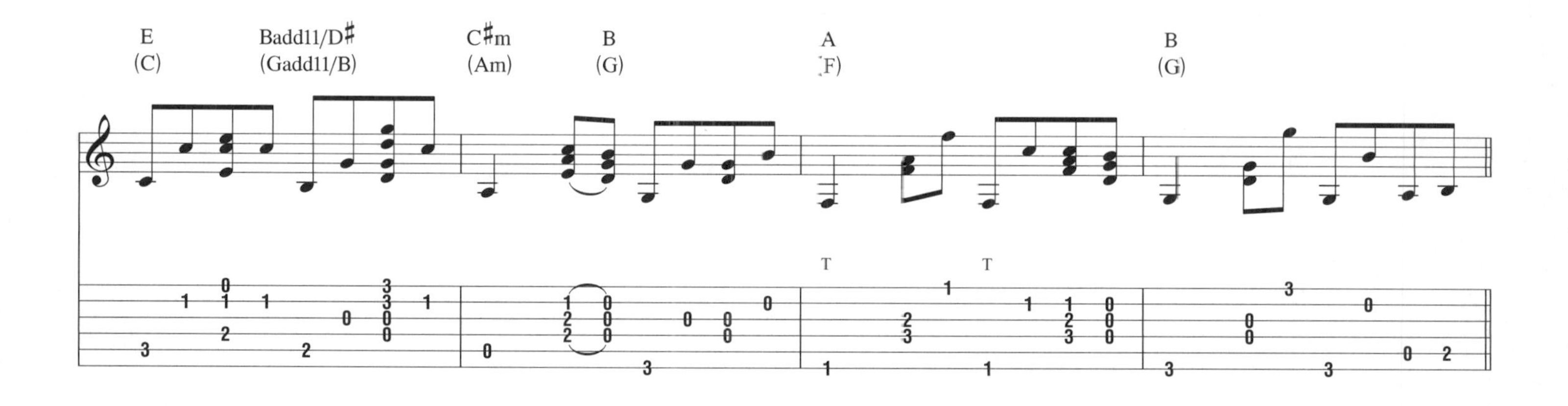

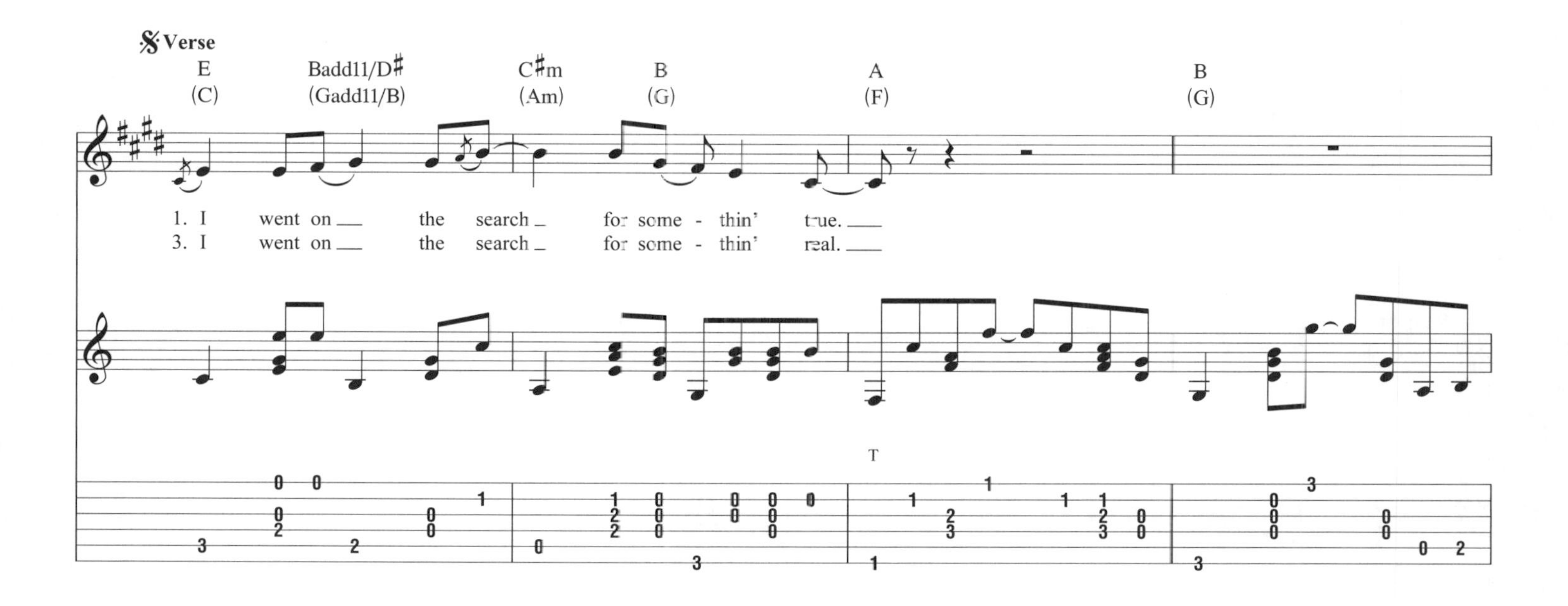

E (C) Badd11/D# (Gadd11/B) C#m (Am) B (G) A (F) B (G)
I was al - most there when I found you.
Trad-ed what I know for how I feel.
But the
E (C) Badd11/D# (Gadd11/B) C#m (Am) B (G) A (F)
Soon - er than my fate was wrote, a per - fect blade, it slit
ceil - in' and the walls col - lapsed, up - on the dark - ness I
B (G) E (C) Badd11/D# (Gadd11/B) C#m (Am) B (G)
my throat, and beads of lust re - leased in - to the air.
was trapped. And as the last of breath was drawn from me,
To Coda 1
A (F) B (G) A (F) B (G)
When I a - woke, you were stand - in' there.
w/ pick

Interlude
E (C)
Badd11/D♯ (Gadd11/B)
C♯m (Am)
B (G)
A (F)
B (G)
w/ pick & fingers
T
Verse
2. I was on the mend when I fell through. The
Rhy. Fig. 1
End Rhy. Fig. 1
w/ pick
sky a - round was an - y - thing but blue. I

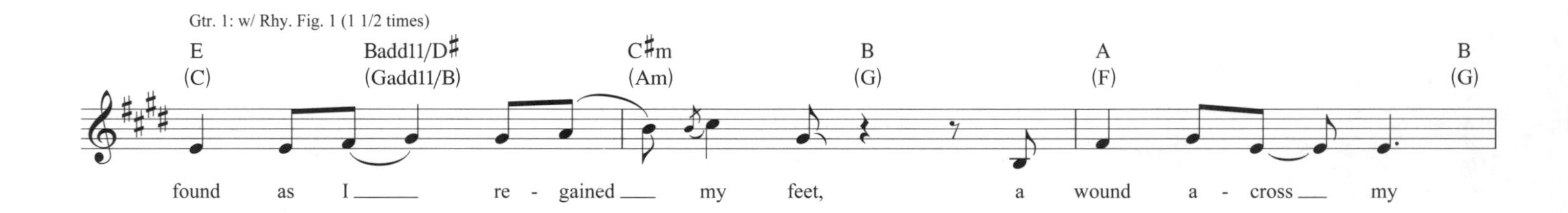
Gtr. 1: w/ Rhy. Fig. 1 (1 1/2 times)
E (C) Badd11/D♯ (Gadd11/B) C♯m (Am) B (G) A (F) B (G)
found as I re - gained my feet, a wound a - cross my

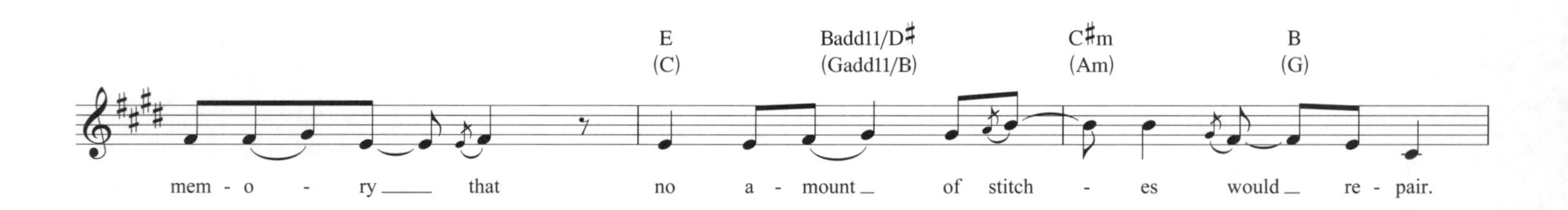
E (C) Badd11/D♯ (Gadd11/B) C♯m (Am) B (G)
mem - o - ry that no a - mount of stitch - es would re - pair.

A (F) B (G) A (F) B (G)
But I a-woke and you were stand - in'
Gtr. 1
T T T

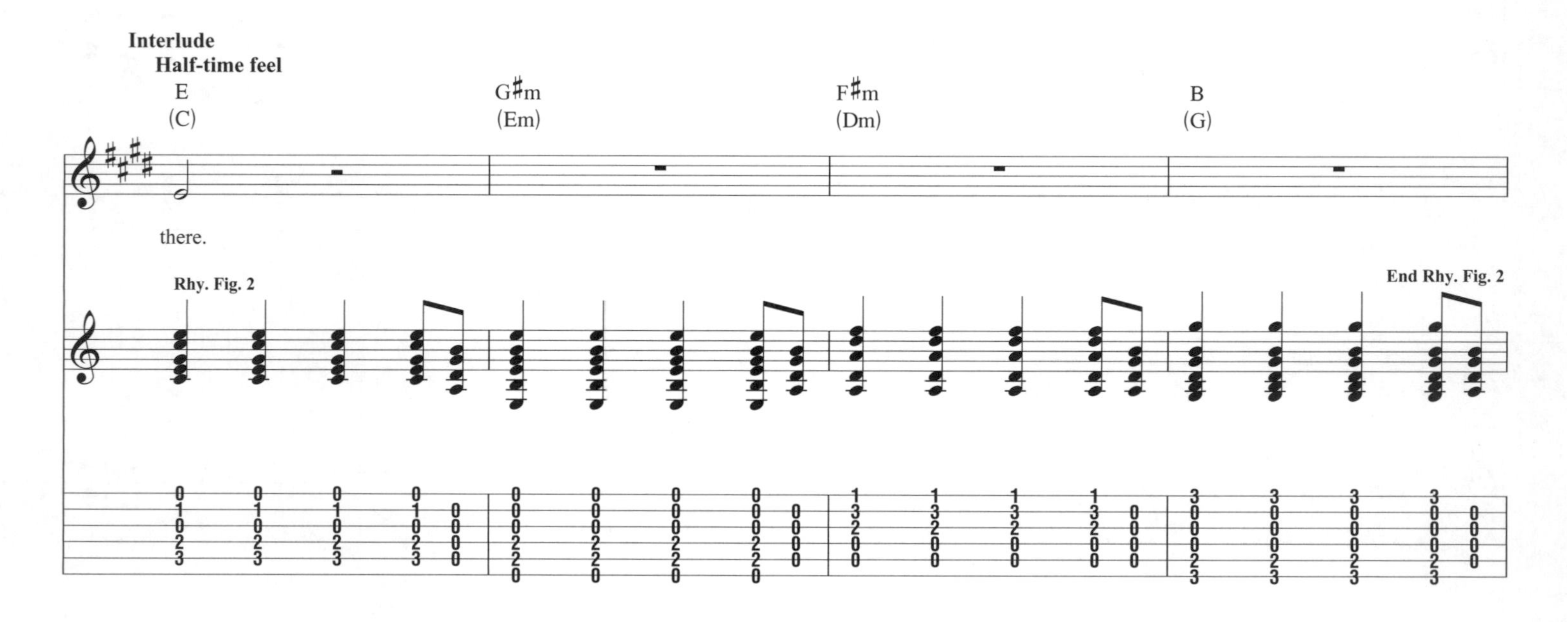
Interlude
Half-time feel
E (C) G♯m (Em) F♯m (Dm) B (G)
there.
Rhy. Fig. 2
End Rhy. Fig. 2

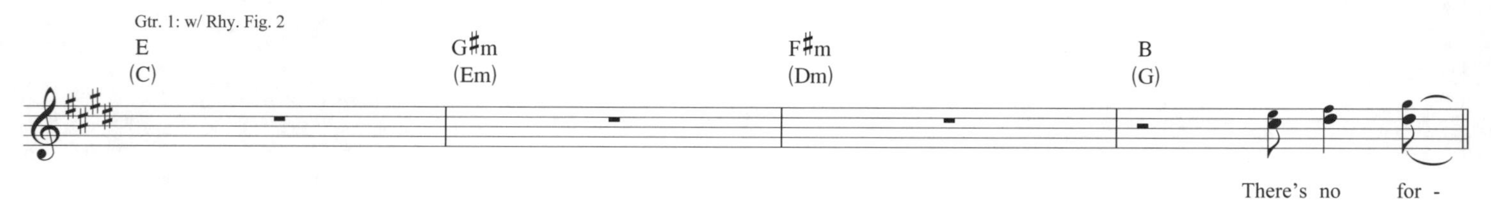
Gtr. 1: w/ Rhy. Fig. 2
E (C) G♯m (Em) F♯m (Dm) B (G)
There's no for -

𝄋𝄋 Chorus
2nd time, Gtr. 1: w/ Rhy. Fig. 4 (3 1/2 times)
E (C) B6add11/D♯ (G6add11/B) C♯m (Am) B (G) A (F) B (G)
- tune at the end of the road that has no end. There's no re - turn -
Rhy. Fig. 3
End Rhy. Fig. 3
Gtr. 1
T

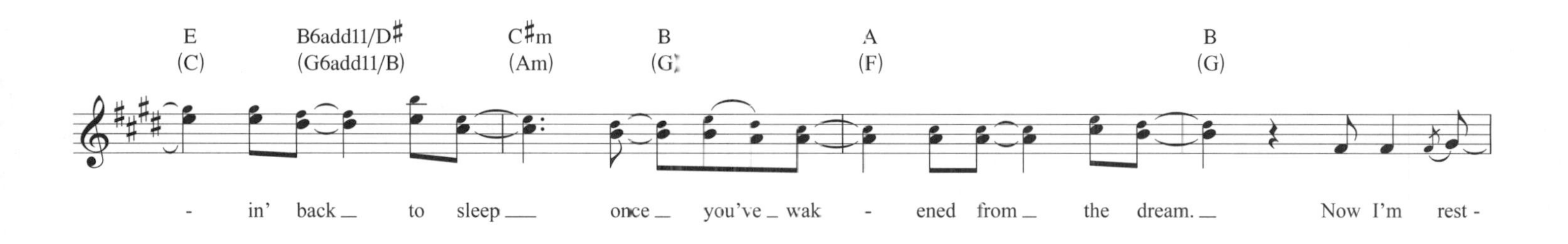

Gtr. 1: w/ Rhy. Fig. 3 (2 times)
E (C) B6add11/D♯ (G6add11/B) C♯m (Am) B (G) A (F) B (G)
- ing to the spoils once you've spoiled the thought of them. There's no fall -

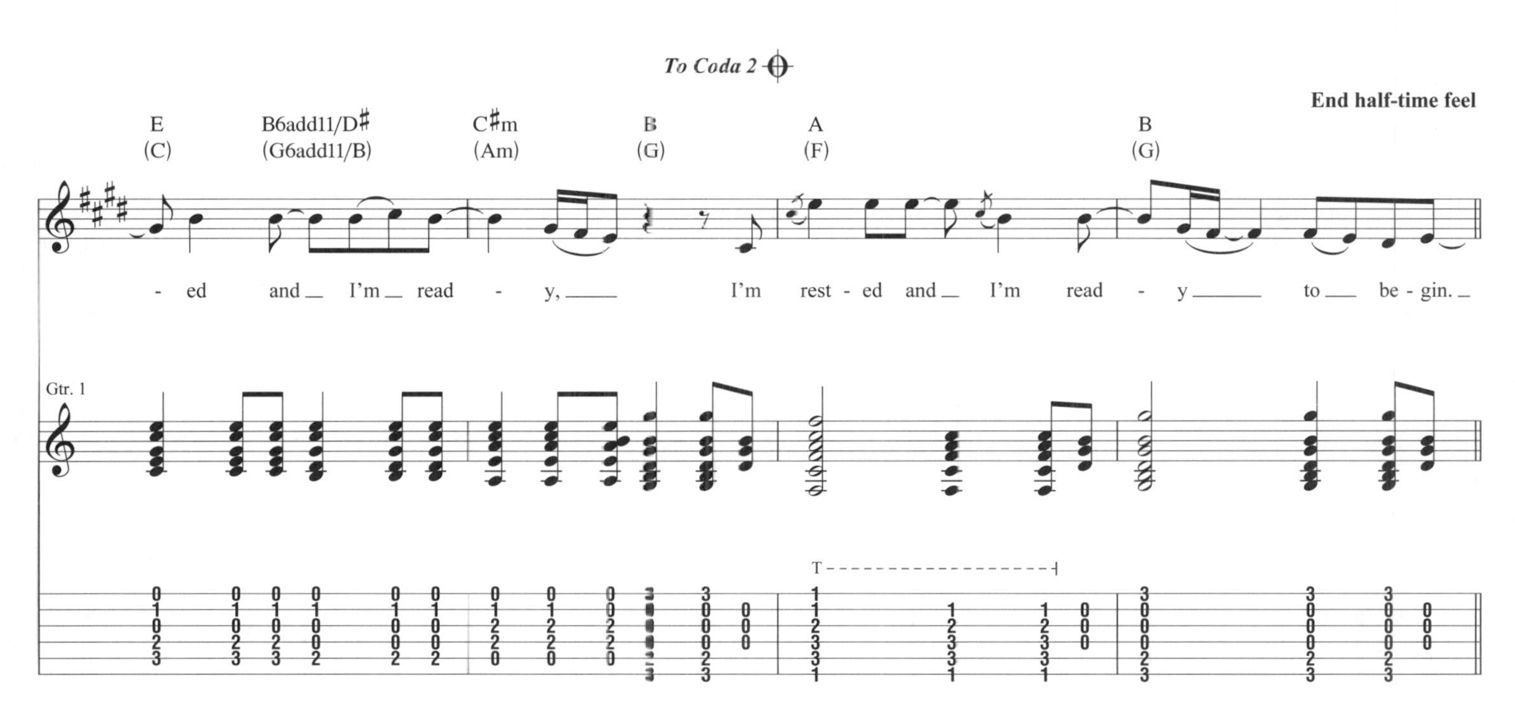

E (C) B6add11/D♯ (G6add11/B) C♯m (Am) B (G) A (F) B (G)
- in' back to sleep once you've wak - ened from the dream. Now I'm rest -
To Coda 2
End half-time feel
E (C) B6add11/D♯ (G6add11/B) C♯m (Am) B (G) A (F) B (G)
- ed and I'm read - y, I'm rest - ed and I'm read - y to be - gin.
Gtr. 1
T

Interlude
E
(C)
Badd11/D♯
(Gadd11/B)
C♯m
(Am)
B
(G)
A
(F)
B
(G)
I'm read - y to be - gin.
D.S. al Coda 1
Coda 1
A
(F)
B
(G)
Half-time feel
E
(C)
B6add11/D♯
(G6add11/B)
light broke in and brought me to my feet.
Rhy. Fig. 4
C♯m
(Am)
B
(G)
A
(F)
B
(G)
D.S.S. al Coda 2
There's no for -
End Rhy. Fig. 4

Coda 2
Gtr. 1: w/ Rhy. Fig. 4 (last 2 meas.)
A
(F)
B
(G)
rest - ed and I'm read - y. Yeah, I'm rest -
Gtr. 1: w/ Rhy. Fig. 4 (1 1/2 times)
E
(C)
B6add11/D♯
(G6add11/B)
C♯m
(Am)
B
(G)
A
(F)
- ed and I'm read - y, I'm rest - ed and I'm read -
- y. Yeah, I'm rest - ed and I'm read - y, I'm
rest - ed and I'm read - y to be - gin.
Gtr. 1
Outro
Gtr. 1: w/ Rhy. Fig. 2
G♯m
(Em)
F♯m
(Dm)
I'm read - y to be - gin.
poco rit.

from *Emotionalism*

I Would Be Sad

Words and Music by Scott Avett, Seth Avett and Robert Crawford

Fm (Em) Db (C) Eb7 (D7)
sad be - cause I got left by a girl that I a - dore.
Ab (G) Ab/G (G/F#) Fm (Em) Db (C)
I would be sad be - cause the love I had be - fore.
Ab (G)
Verse
Ab (G)
1. I meant what I said
End Rhy. Fig. 1
Rhy. Fig. 2
Ab/G (G/F#) Fm (Em)
when I said I would set - tle down with you. Al -

D♭
(C)
E♭7
(D7)
though I know it's not some - thing that you were ask - ing me
End Rhy. Fig. 2
A♭
(G)
A♭/G
(G/F♯)
to do. And I know we are young, but we won't al -
Fm
(Em)
D♭
(C)
3
- ways be, so mar - ry me. Let's not be that pre -
E♭7
(D7)
dict - a - ble young cou - ple, chang - ing, mov - ing on. But

*Tap on lower bout of guitar with pick-hand thumb.

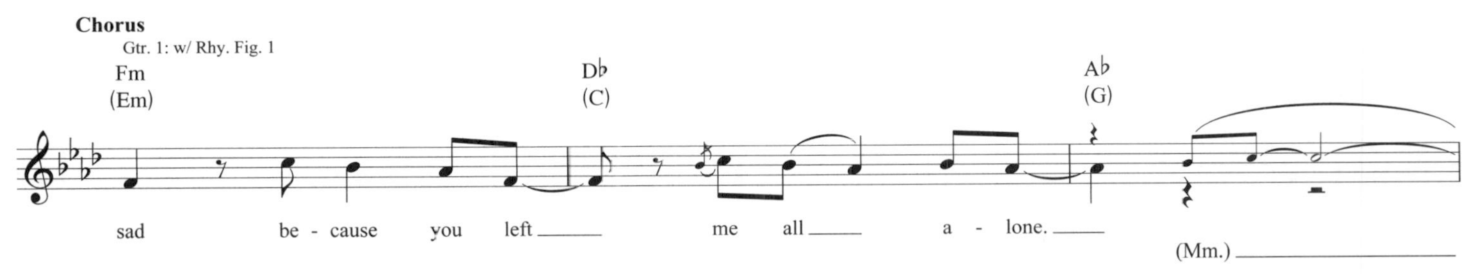

Ab/G
(G/F#)
Fm
(Em)
Db
(C)
I would be sad be - cause the lies that you had told.
Ab
(G)
Ab/G
(G/F#)
Fm
(Em)
(Mm.)
I would be sad be - cause I got
Db
(C)
Eb7
(D7)
Ab
(G)
Ab/G
(G/F#)
left by a girl that I a - dore. I would be
Fm
(Em)
Db
(C)
Ab
(G)
sad for all the love I had be - fore.
Verse
Ab
(G)
Cm
(Bm)
2. I meant what I said when I said I would
Gtr. 1
Db
(C)
Eb7
(D7)
Ab
(G)
re - ar - range my plans and change for you.

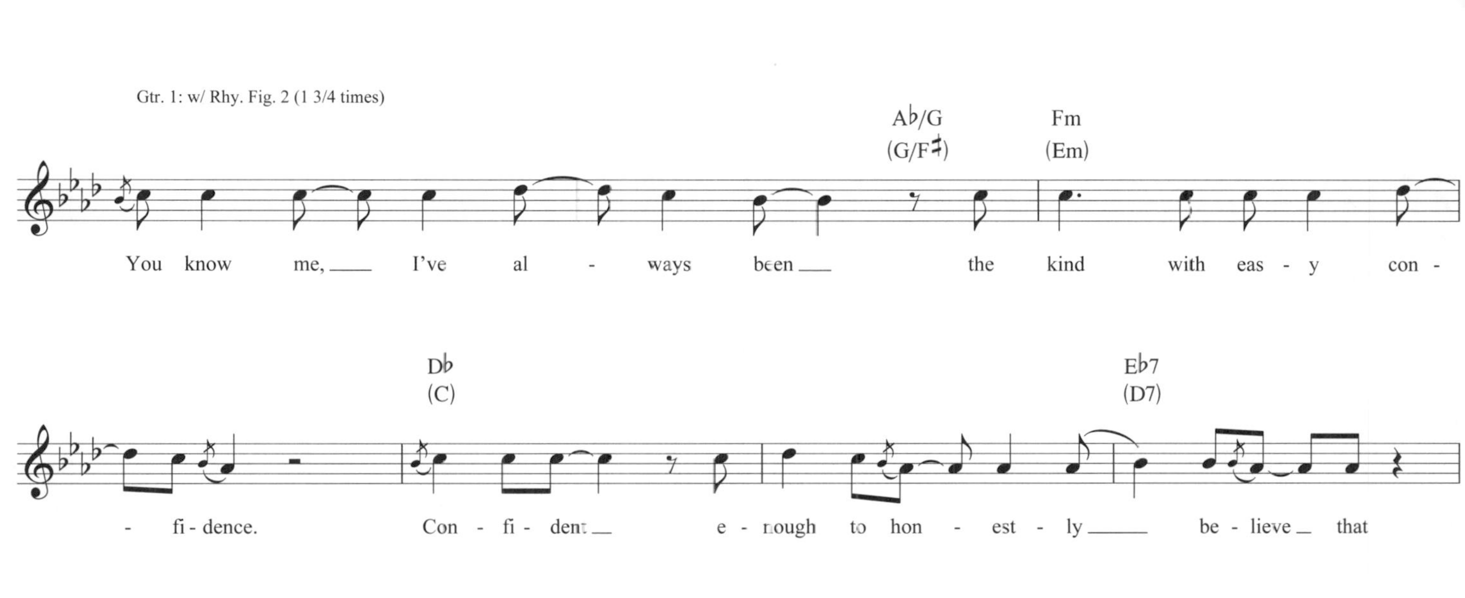
Gtr. 1: w/ Rhy. Fig. 2 (1 3/4 times)
A♭/G
(G/F♯)
Fm
(Em)
You know me, I've al - ways been the kind with eas - y con -

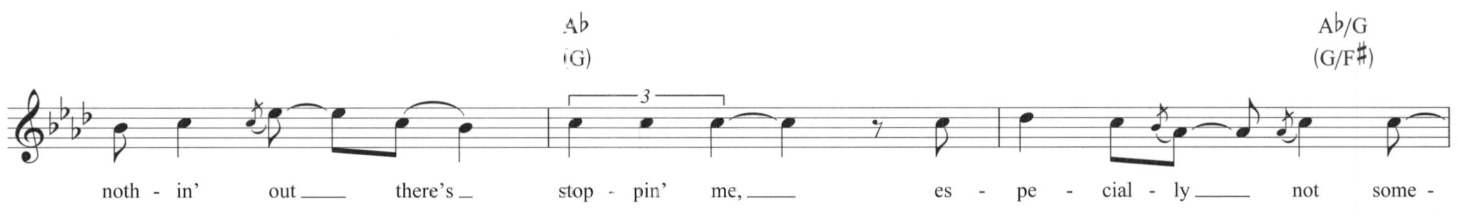
D♭
(C)
E♭7
(D7)
- fi - dence. Con - fi - dent e - nough to hon - est - ly be - lieve that

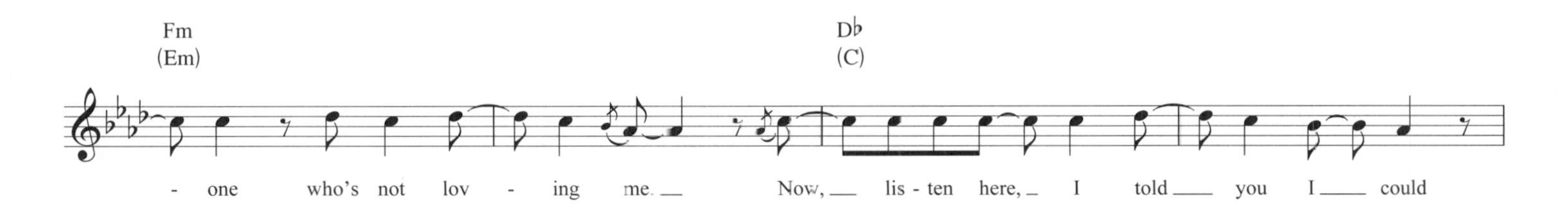
A♭
(G)
A♭/G
(G/F♯)
noth - in' out there's stop - pin' me, es - pe - cial - ly not some -

Fm
(Em)
D♭
(C)
- one who's not lov - ing me. Now, lis - ten here, I told you I could
E♭7
(D7)
D♭
(C)
live on with - out lov - ing you. I was bluff - in' then
Gtr. 1
*As before

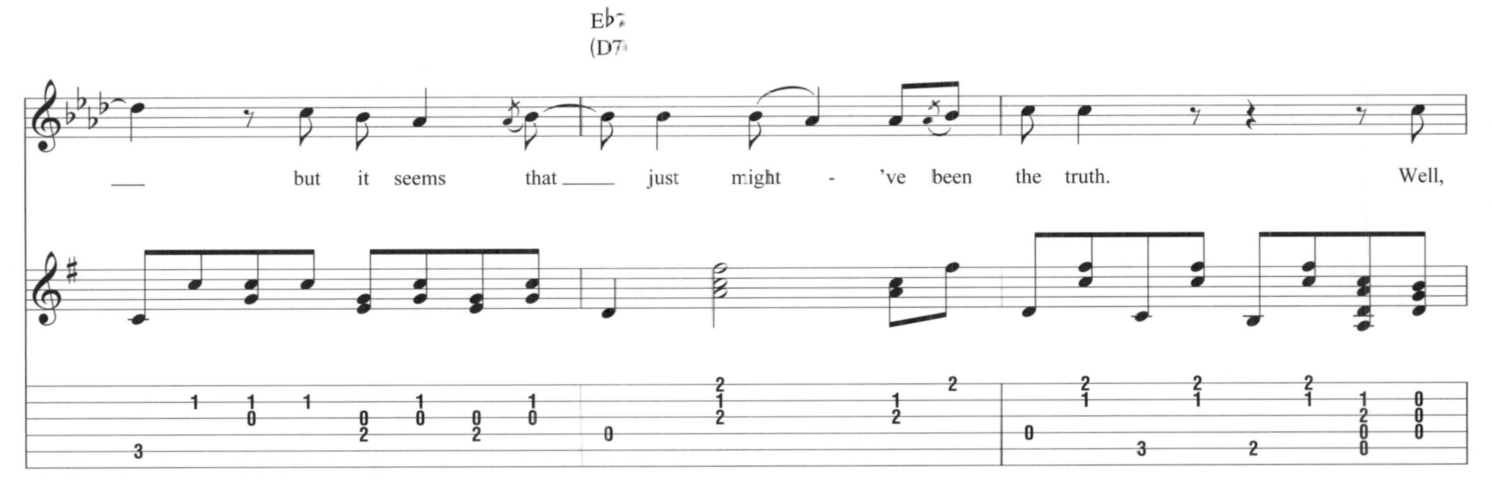
E♭7
(D7)
but it seems that just might - 've been the truth. Well,

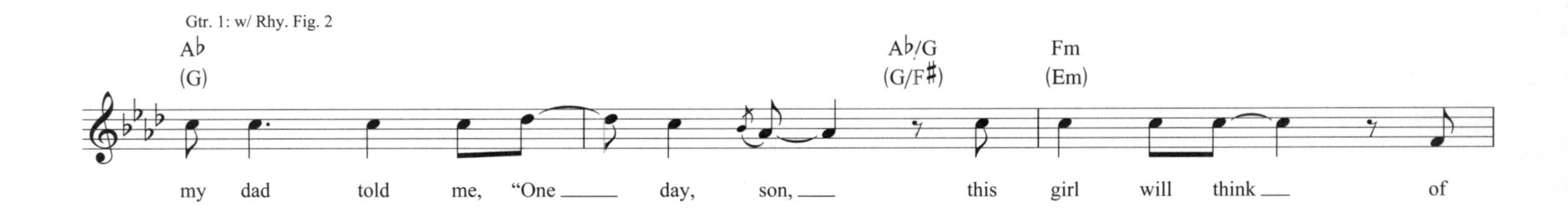
Gtr. 1: w/ Rhy. Fig. 2
A♭
(G)
A♭/G
(G/F♯)
Fm
(Em)
my dad told me, "One day, son, this girl will think of

D♭
(C)
what she's done. And hurt - ing you will be the first of

E♭7
(D7)
Gtr. 1: w/ Rhy. Fig. 3
A♭
(G)
man - y more re - grets to come." And he said, "If she does -

A♭/G
(G/F♯)
Fm
(Em)
n't call, then it's her fault and it's her loss." I say

D♭
(C)
E♭7
(D7)
it's not that sim - ple, see? But then a - gain, it just

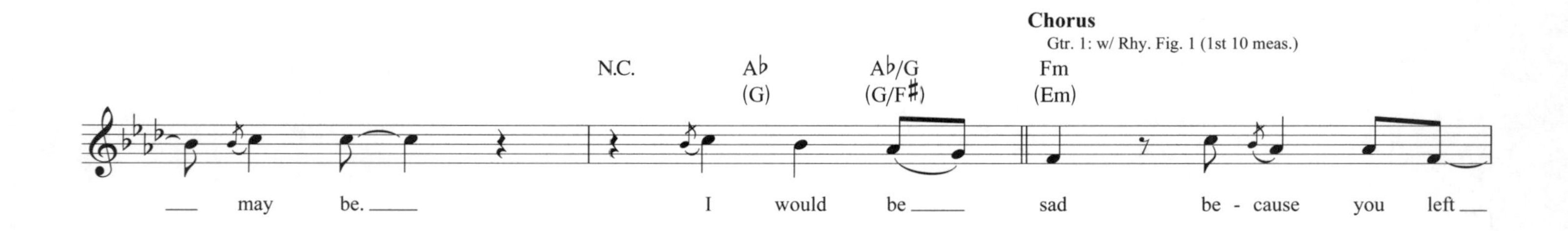
Chorus
Gtr. 1: w/ Rhy. Fig. 1 (1st 10 meas.)
N.C.
A♭
(G)
A♭/G
(G/F♯)
Fm
(Em)
may be. I would be sad be - cause you left

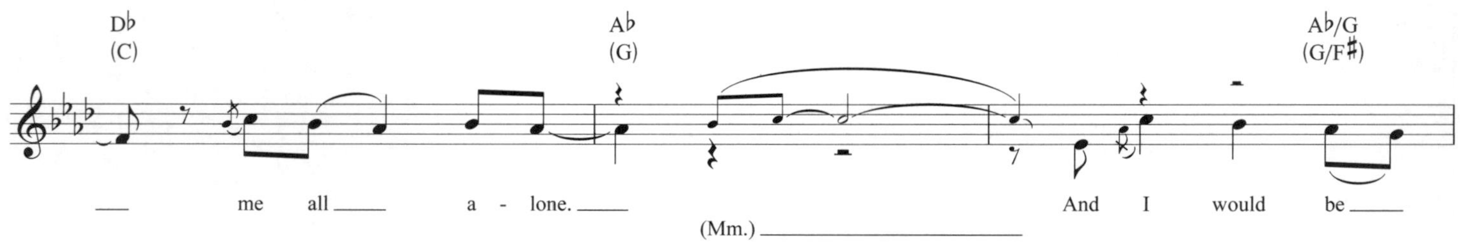
D♭
(C)
A♭
(G)
A♭/G
(G/F♯)
me all a - lone. And I would be
(Mm.)

Fm (Em) Db (C) Ab (G)
sad for all the lies that you have told me.
(Mm.)
Ab/G (G/F#) Fm (Em) Db (C)
And I would be sad be - cause I got left by a girl
Eb7 (D7) Ab (G) Ab/G (G/F#) Fm (Em)
that I a - dore. I would be sad for all the love
Gtr. 1
Db (C) Ab (G)
I had be - fore.
rit.
I would be
rit.
Outro
Fm (Em) Db (C) Ab (G)
sad for all the love I had be - fore.

from *The Carpenter*

Live and Die

Words and Music by Scott Avett, Seth Avett and Robert Crawford

Gtr. 1: Double drop D, capo IV
(low to high) D-A-D-G-B-D

Gtr. 2: Capo IV

*Banjo arr. for gtr.

**Symbols in parentheses represent chord names respective to capoed guitar. Symbols above reflect actual sounding chords. Capoed fret is "0" in tab. Chord symbols reflect implied harmony.

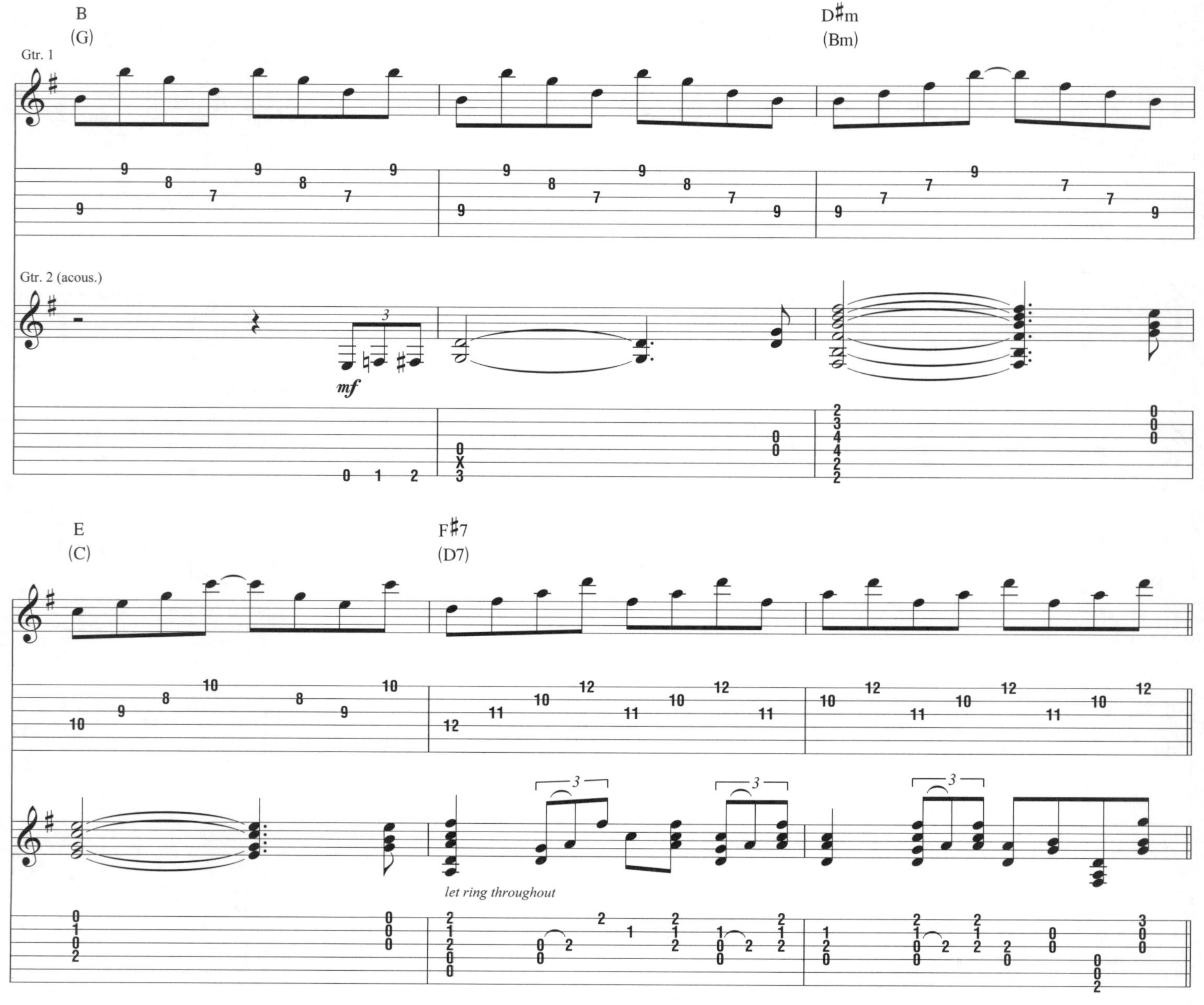

Verse
B
(G)
D♯m
(Bm)
E
(C)
B
(G)
1. All it - 'll take is just one mo - ment and

G♯m
(Em)
E
(C)
F♯7
(D7)
you can say good - bye to how we had it planned.

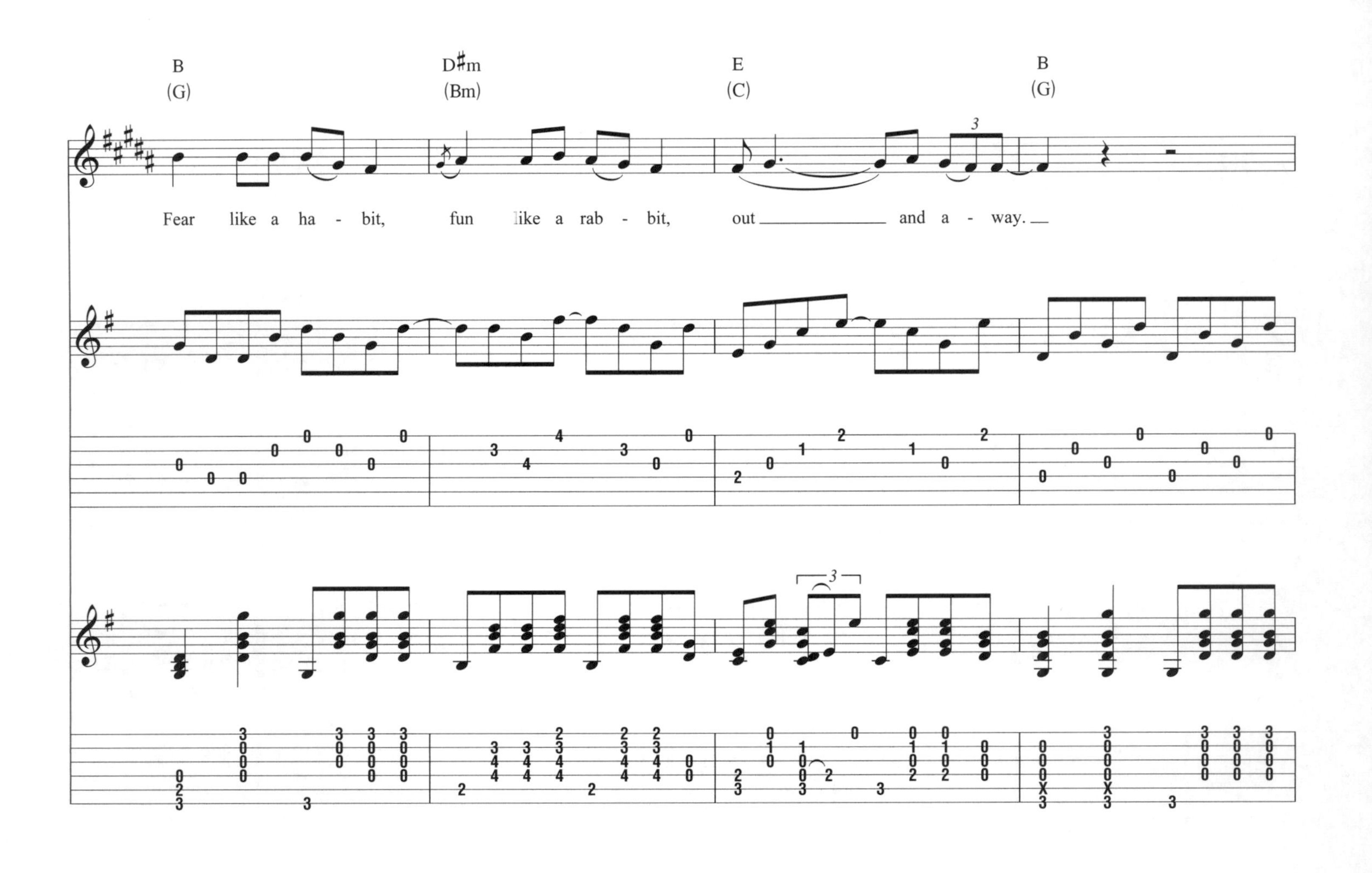
B
(G)
D#m
(Bm)
E
(C)
B
(G)
Fear like a ha - bit, fun like a rab - bit, out and a - way.

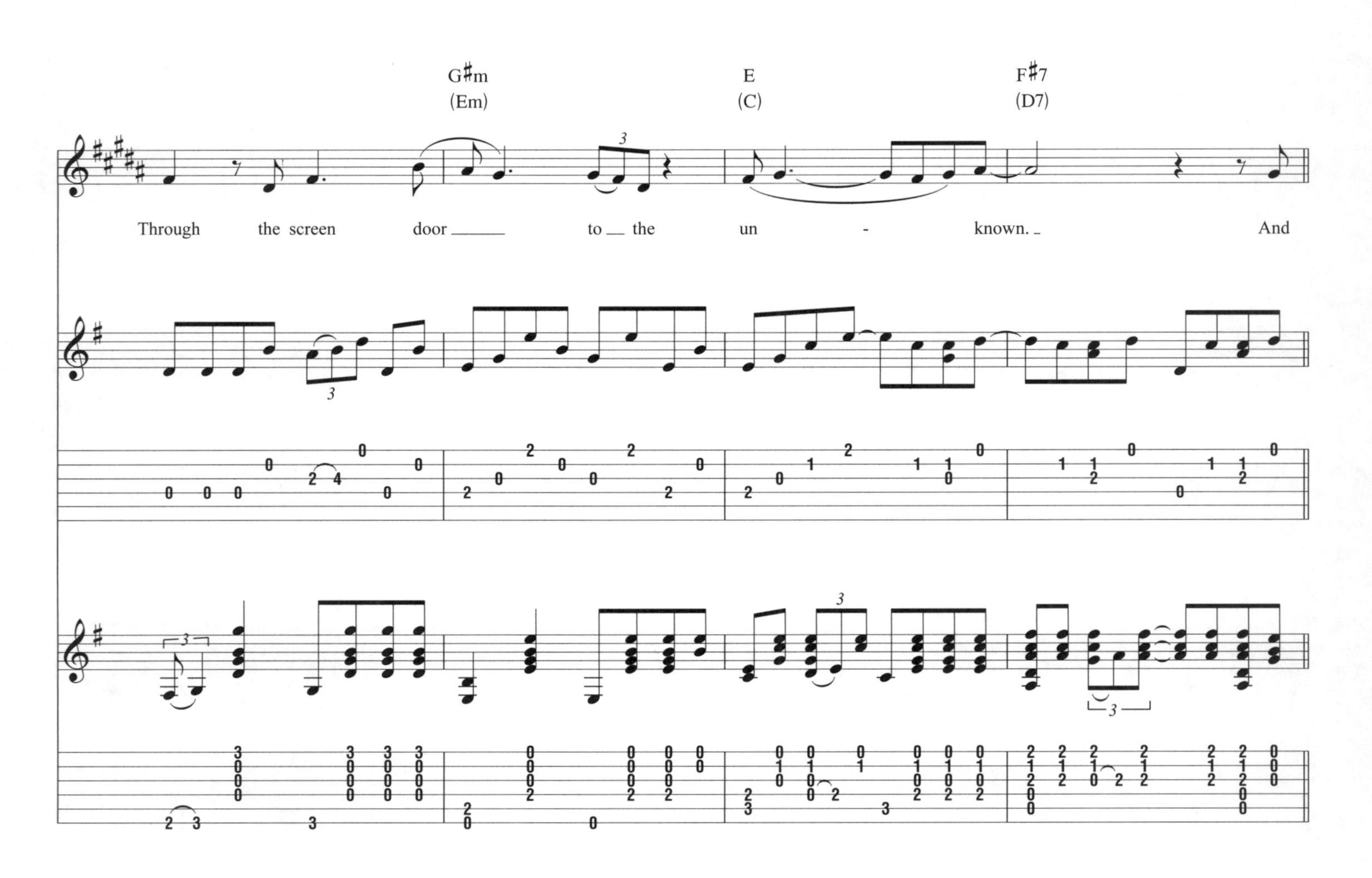
G#m
(Em)
E
(C)
F#7
(D7)
Through the screen door to the un - known. And

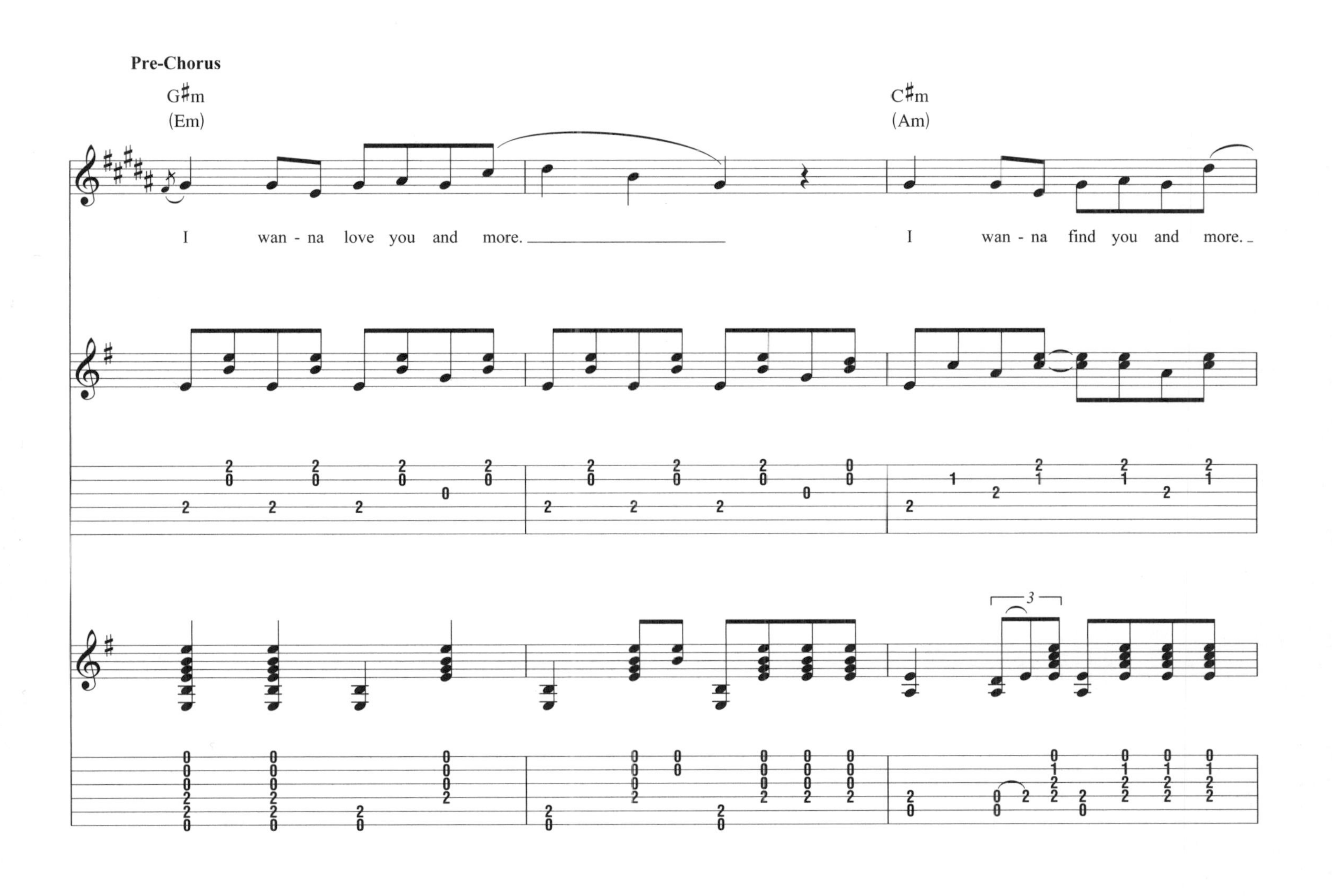
Pre-Chorus
G#m
(Em)
C#m
(Am)
I wan - na love you and more.
I wan - na find you and more.

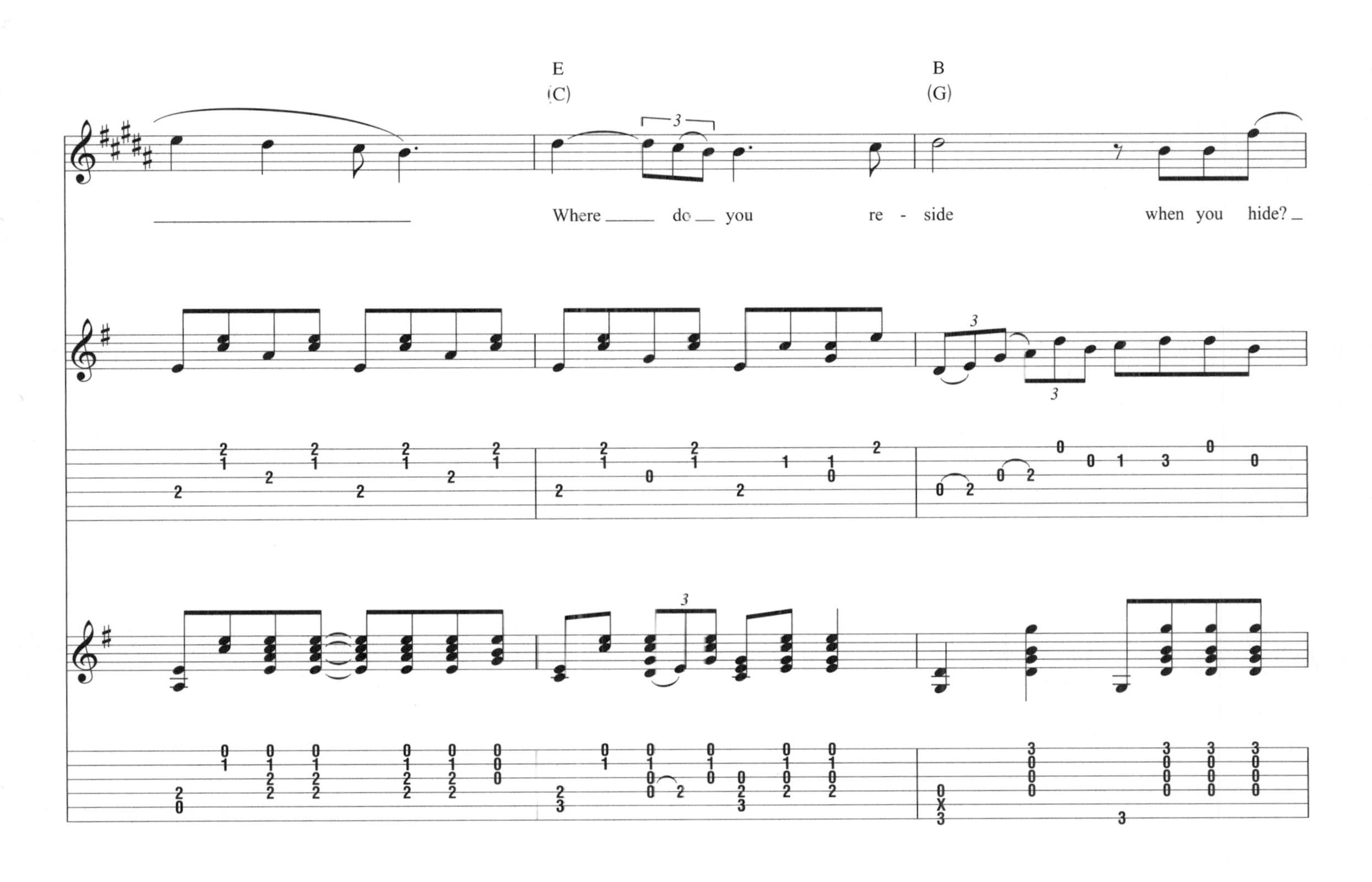
E
(C)
B
(G)
Where do you re - side when you hide?

D♯m
(Bm)
E
(C)
G♯m
(Em)
How can I find you? 'Cause I wan - na send you and more.
C♯m
(Am)
I wan - na tempt you and more.
Gtr. 3 (elec.)
mf
w/ slight dist.
w/ slide
Gtr. 1
Gtr. 2

E
(C)
E
(G)
D♯m
(Bm)
Can ___ you _ tell that I am a - live? ___ Let me prove _
E
(C)
it. You and I, ___

Chorus
B
(G)
G♯m
(Em)
C♯m
(Am)
F♯7
(D7)
we're the same.
Live and die,
we're the same.
Hear my voice,
know my name.
You and I,
let ring
we're the same.

Verse
B
(G)
D#m
(Bm)
Gtr. 3 tacet
E
(C)
2. Live like a phar - aoh, sing like a spar - row, an - y - way.
B
(G)
G#m
(Em)
E
(C)
E - ven if there is no land or love in sight.
Gtr. 1
Gtr. 2

F#7
(D7)
B
(G)
D#m
(Bm)
We bloom like ros - es, lead like Mos - es,
Gtr. 3
Gtr. 1
Gtr. 2
E
(C)
B
(G)
out and a - way.
Through the bit - ter crowd
steady gliss.

G♯m
(Em)
E
(C)
F♯7
(D7)
to the day - light. And
Pre-Chorus
G♯m
(Em)
C♯m
(Am)
I wan - na love you and more.
I wan - na find you and more.

E
(C)
B
(G)
Can you tell that I am a - live?
D♯m
(Bm)
E
(C)
Let me prove it to you.
You and I,

Chorus
B
(G)
G#m
(Em)
C#m
(Am)
F#7
(D7)
we're the same.
Live and die,
we're the same.
And you re - joice,
Rhy. Fig. 1
End Rhy. Fig. 1
Gtr. 1: w/ Rhy. Fig. 1 (2 1/2 times)
I com-plain, but you and I,
we're the same.
Live and die,
we're the same.
You and I,
Gtr. 3
let ring
Gtr. 2

C♯m
(Am)
F♯7
(D7)
B
(G)
G♯m
(Em)
we're the same.
Hear my voice,
know my name.
You and I,
Gtr. 3
Gtr. 2
C♯m
(Am)
F♯7
(D7)
we're the same.
let ring
Gtr. 1

Interlude

Gtr. 3 tacet
B
(G)
D♯m
(Bm)
E
(C)
Gtr. 3
Gtr. 1
Gtr. 4 (elec.)
mf
w/ dist.
Gtr. 2
B
(G)
G♯m
(Em)
Gtr. 1
Gtr. 4
Gtr. 2

E
(C)
F♯7
(D7)
B
(G)
Gtr. 3
Gtr. 1
let ring
Gtr. 4
Gtr. 2
Gtr. 4 tacet
D♯m
(Bm)
E
(C)
Gtr. 3
Gtr. 1
Gtr. 2

B
(G)
let ring
let ring
G♯m
(Em)
E
(C)
F♯7
(D7)

Pre-Chorus

Gtr. 3 tacet
G♯m
(Em)
C♯m
(Am)
I wan - na love you and more.
I wan - na find you and more.
Gtr. 3
Gtr. 1
Gtr. 4
Gtr. 2

E
(C)
B
(G)
Where do you re - side when you hide?
Gtr. 1
Gtr. 4
Gtr. 2
D♯m
(Bm)
E
(C)
G♯m
(Em)
How can I find you? 'Cause I wan - na send you and more.
Harm.

C♯m
(Am)
I wan - na tempt you and more.
Gtr. 3
Gtr. 1
Gtr. 4
Gtr. 2

E
(C)
B
(G)
D♯m
(Bm)
Can you tell that I am a - live? Let me prove
8va
loco

E
(C)
it.
But you and I,

Chorus
Gtr. 1: w/ Rhy. Fig. 1 (3 1/2 times)
Gtr. 4 tacet
B
(G)
G♯m
(Em)
C♯m
(Am)
F♯7
(D7)
we're the same.
Live and die,
we're the same.
You re - joice,
Gtr. 3
Gtr. 2
I com - plain
but
you and I,
we're the same.
Live and die,

B (G)
G♯m (Em)
C♯m (Am)
F♯7 (D7)
B (G)
G♯m (Em)
we're the same. You and I, we're the same. Hear my voice, know my name. You and I.
let ring
C♯m (Am)
F♯7 (D7)
You and I.
8va
Gtr. 3
Gtr. 1
Gtr. 2

B
(G)
Gtr. 3
8va
loco
Gtr. 1
Gtr. 4
Gtr. 2

from *Carolina Jubilee*

Love Like the Movies

Words and Music by Scott Avett, Seth Avett and Robert Crawford

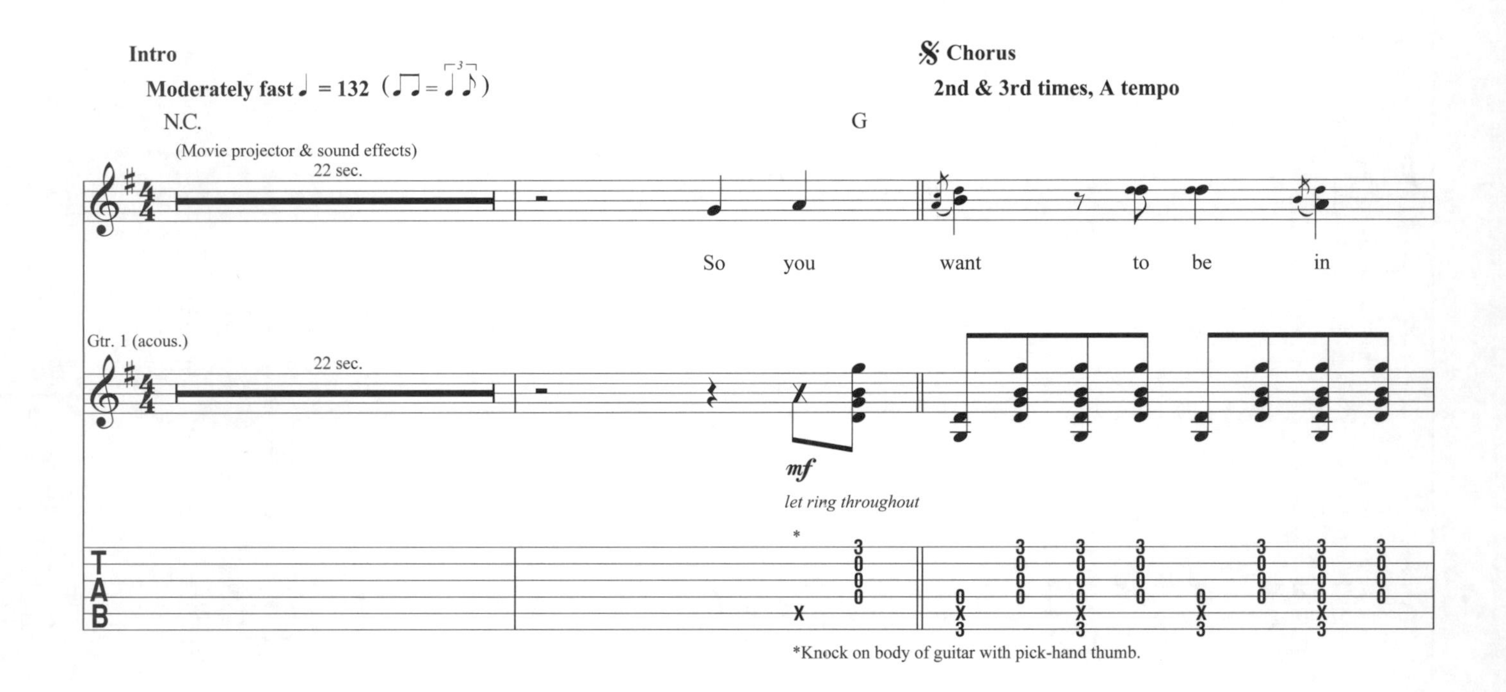

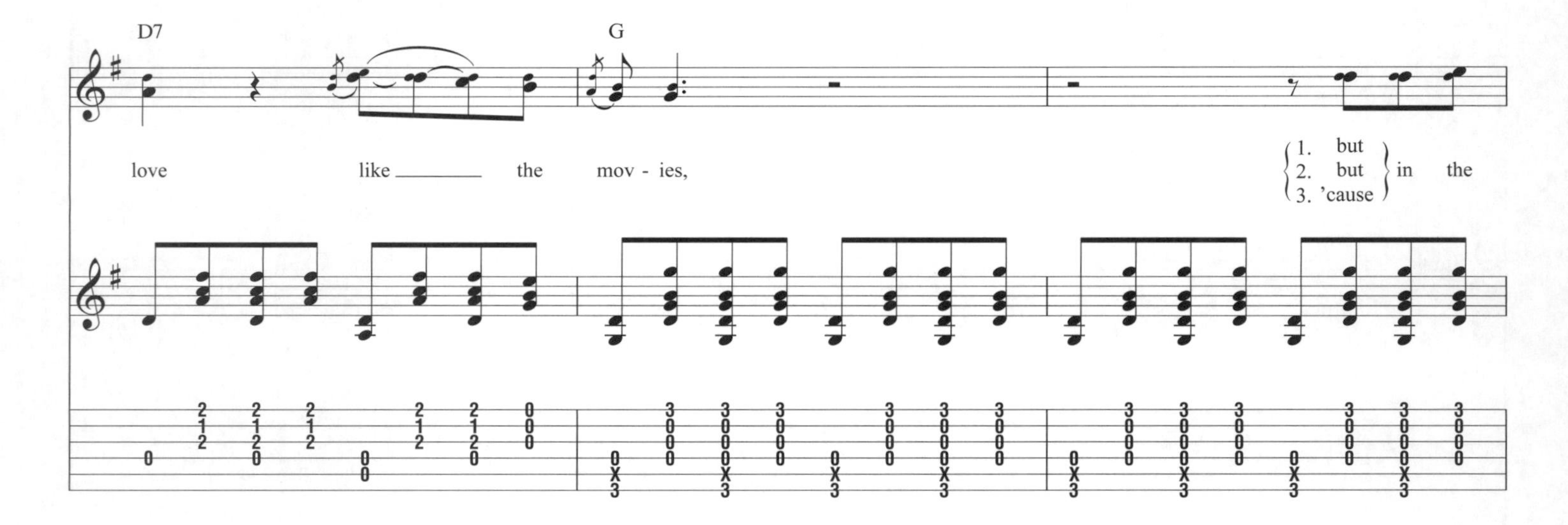

G/F♯
Em
D7
With a twink - le in their eyes,
(Oo, ah,
B7
C
G
D7
they're just say - in' their lines.
And so we can't be in
oo.)
To Coda 2
To Coda 1
C
D7
G
love like the mov - ies
1. Now in the
2. Well, you can

Verse
B7
C
G
mov - ies, they make it, uh, look so per - fect. And in the
Rhy. Fig. 1
End Rhy. Fig. 1
Gtr. 1: w/ Rhy. Fig. 1 (2 times)
B7
C
G
back - ground, they're al - ways play - in' the right song. And in the
B7
C
G
end - in' there's al - ways a res - o - lu - tion. But

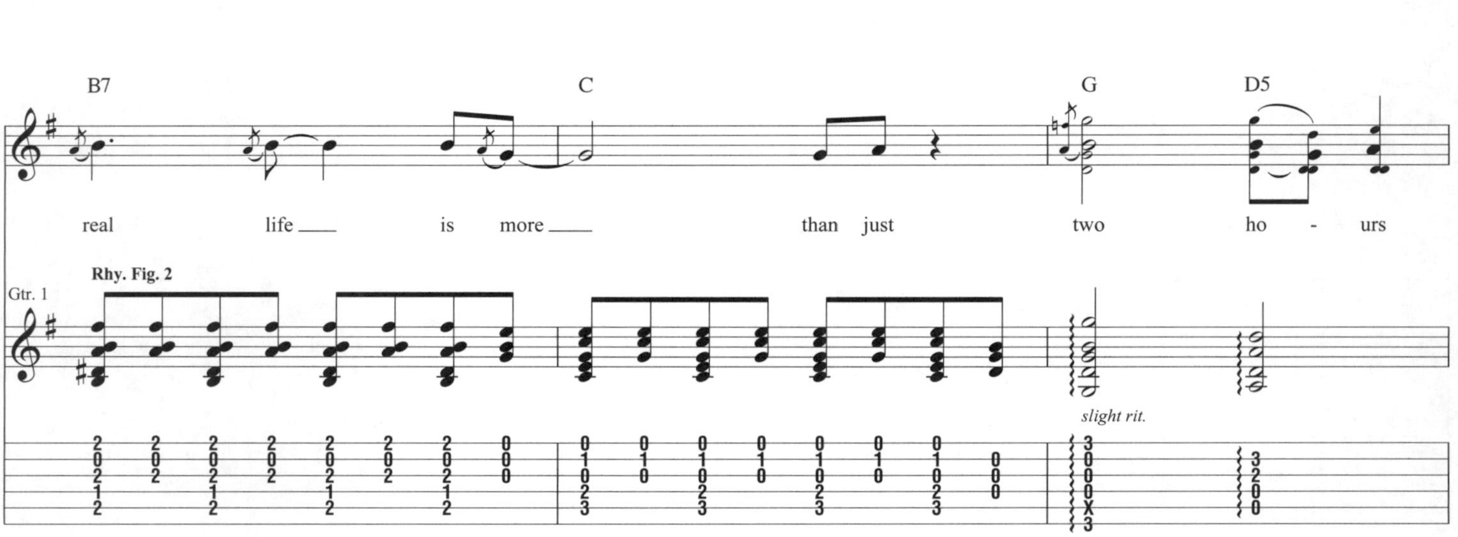
B7
C
G
D5
real life is more than just two ho - urs
Rhy. Fig. 2
Gtr. 1
slight rit.

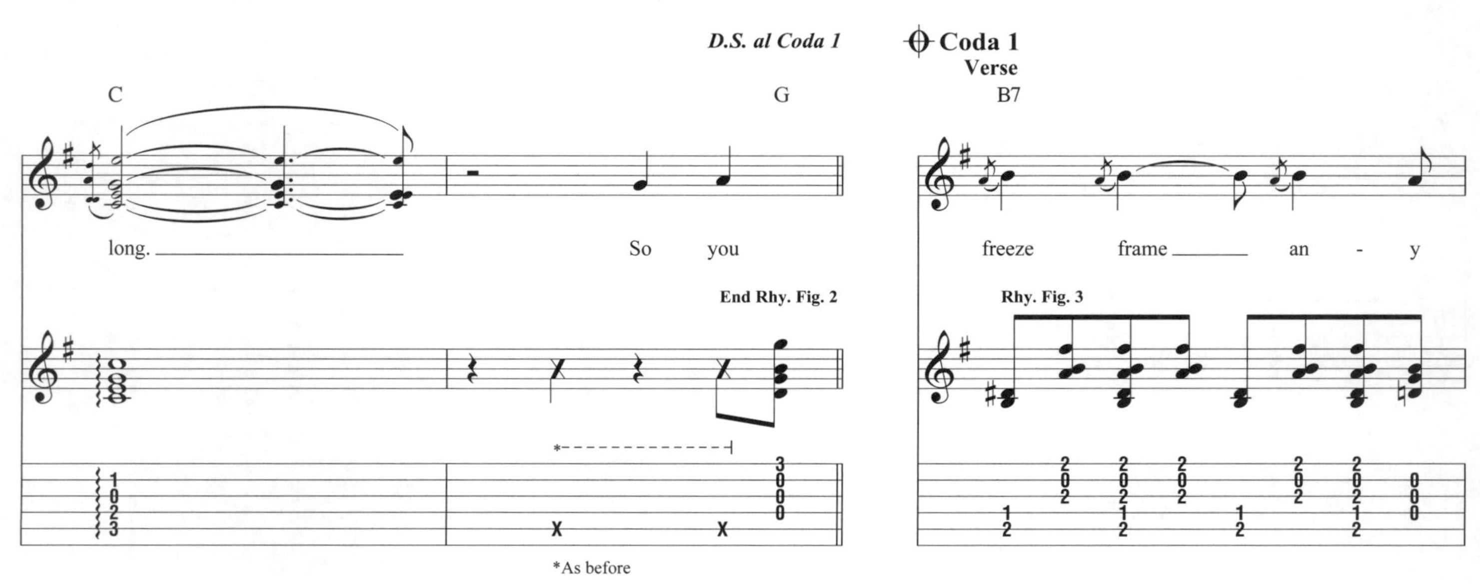
D.S. al Coda 1
Coda 1
Verse
C
G
B7
long. So you freeze frame an - y
End Rhy. Fig. 2
Rhy. Fig. 3
*As before

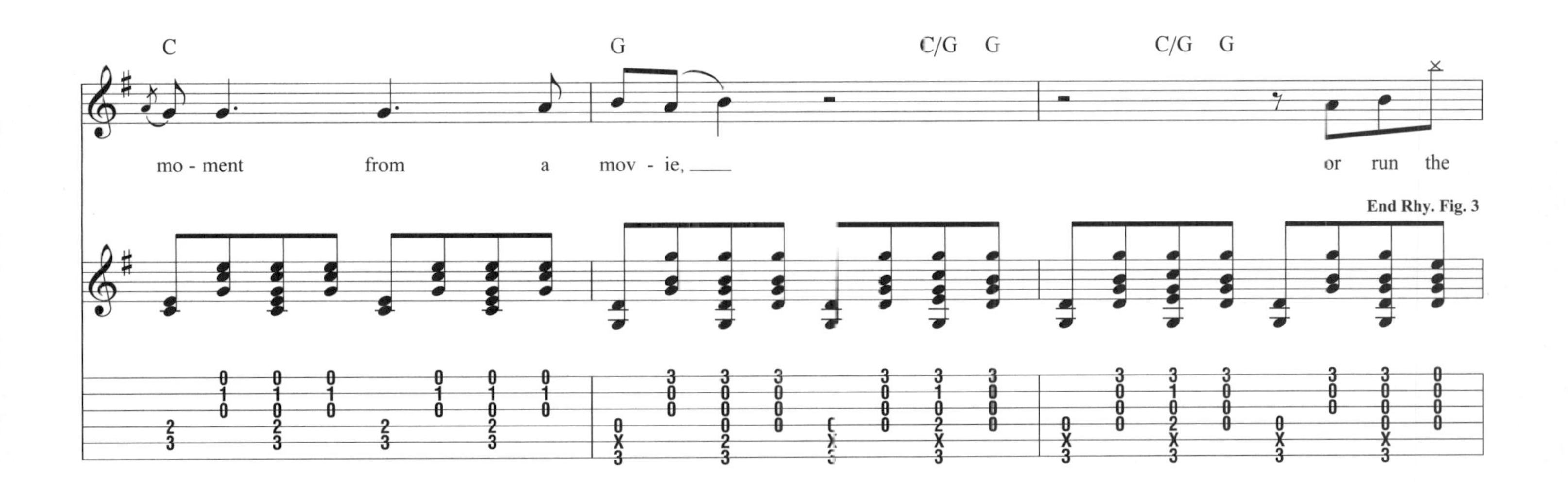

Gtr. 1: w/ Rhy. Fig. 3 (2 times)

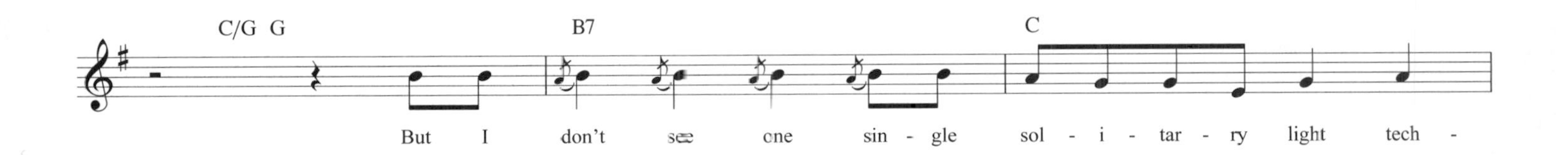

Gtr. 1: w/ Rhy. Fig. 2

D.S. al Coda 2

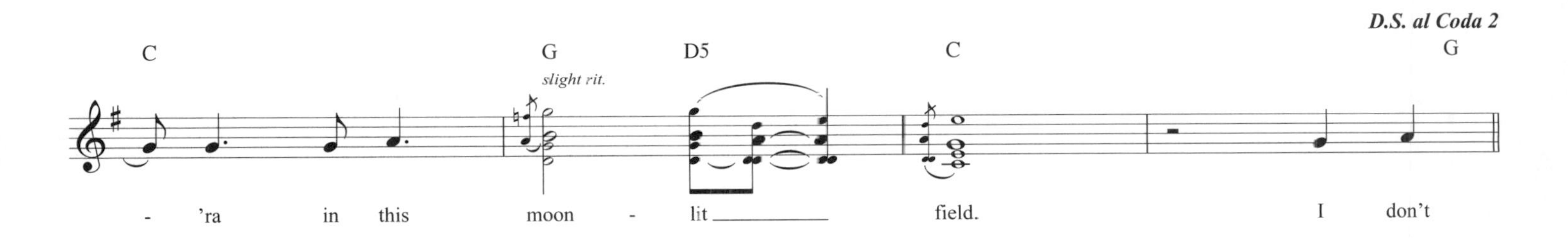

Coda 2

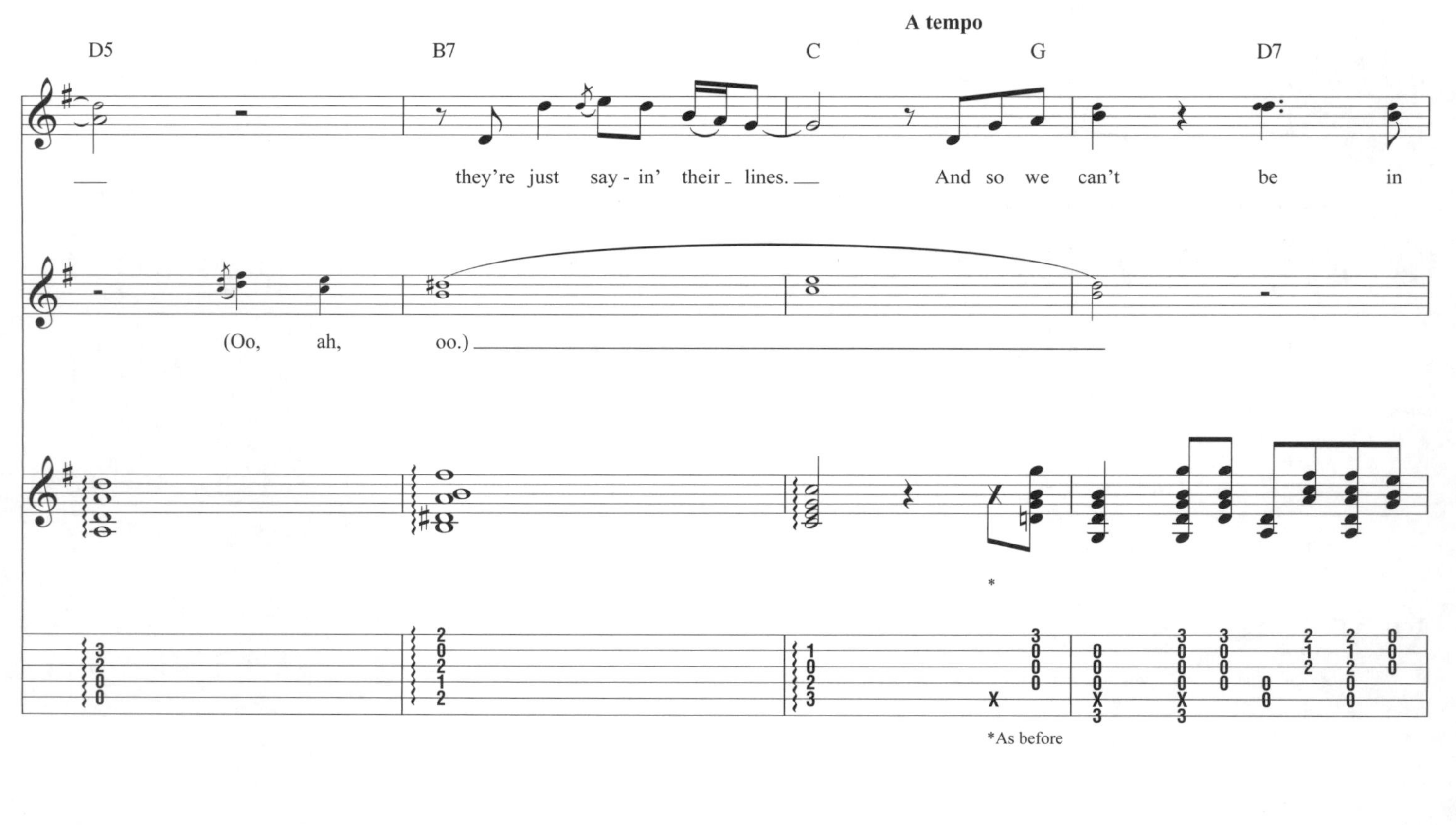
A tempo
D5
B7
C
G
D7
they're just say - in' their lines.
And so we can't be in
(Oo, ah, oo.)
*
*As before

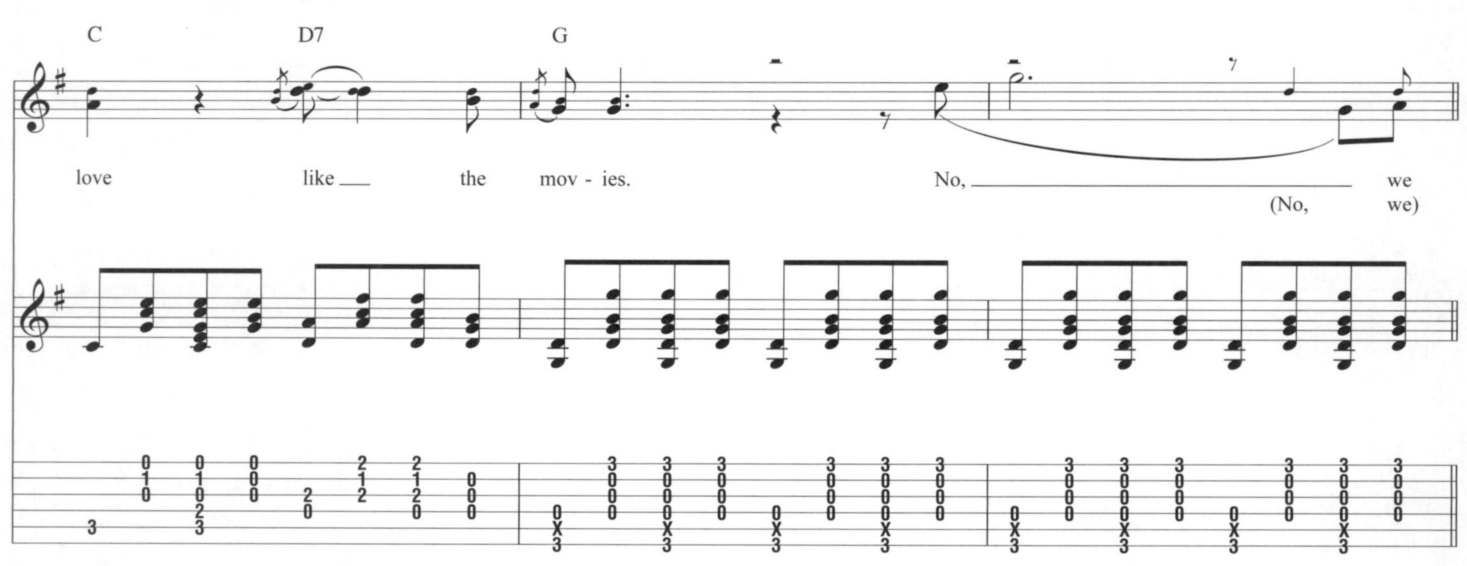
C
D7
G
love like the mov - ies.
No, we
(No, we)

Outro
G5
N.C.
D
N.C.
C
N.C.
D
N.C.
G
can't be in love like the mov - ies.

from *The Second Gleam*

Murder in the City

Words and Music by Scott Avett and Timothy Avett

*Symbols in parentheses represent chord names respective to capoed Gtr. 1.
Symbols in double parentheses represent chord names respective to capoed Gtr. 2.
Symbols above reflect actual sounding chords. Capoed fret is "0" in tab.
Chord symbols reflect implied harmony.

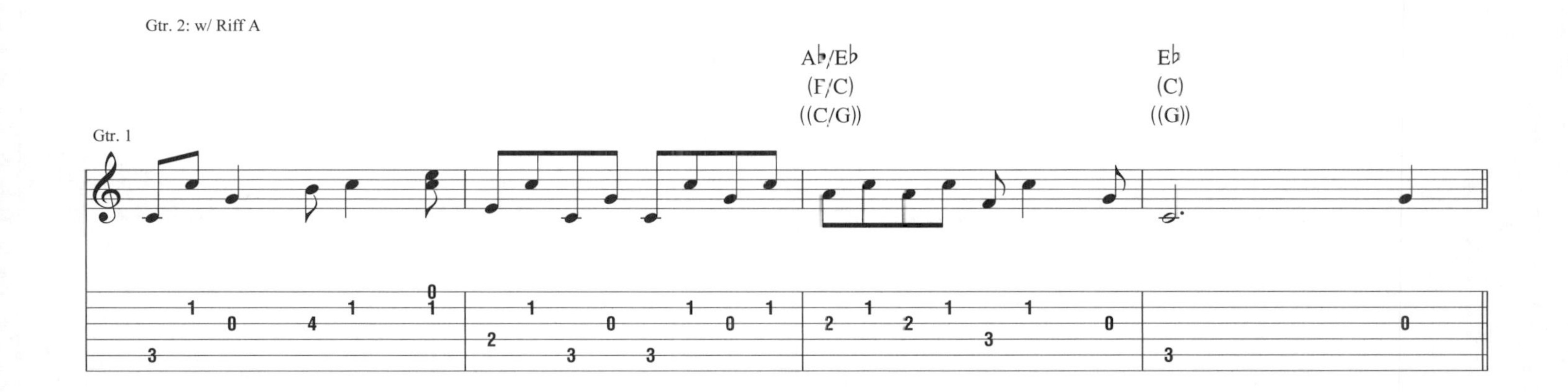

Verse
E♭
(C)
((G))
E♭/D
(C/B)
((G/F♯))
Cm
(Am)
((Em))
B♭
(G)
((D))
A♭
(F)
((C))
B♭
(G)
((D))
E♭
(C)
((G))
1. If I get mur-dered in the cit - y don't go re-veng-in' in my name.
2. I won-der which brother-er is bet - ter, which one our par-ents loved the most.
Riff B
End Riff B
Gtr. 1
Gtr. 2

Gtr. 1: w/ Riff B
E♭/D
(C/B)
((G/F♯))
Cm
(Am)
((Em))
B♭
(G)
((D))
A♭
(F)
((C))
B♭
(G)
((D))
E♭
(C)
((G))
One per-son dead from such is plen - ty. No need to go get locked a-way.
I sure did get in lots of trou - ble. They seemed to let the oth - er go.
Riff C
End Riff C
Gtr. 2

Cm (Am) ((Em))
B♭ (G) ((D))
E♭ (C) ((G))
Cm (Am) ((Em))
B♭ (G) ((D))
When I leave your arms, the things that I think of.
A tear fell from my fa-ther's eyes. I won-dered what my dad would say.
Riff D
Gtr. 1
Riff D1
Gtr. 2
E♭ (C) ((G))
Cm (Am) ((Em))
B♭ (G) ((D))
A♭ (F) ((C))
E♭ (C) ((G))
B♭5 (G5) ((D5))
No need to get o-ver-a-larmed. I'm com-in' home
He said, "I love you and I'm proud of you both in so man-y dif-f'rent ways."
End Riff D
End Riff D1

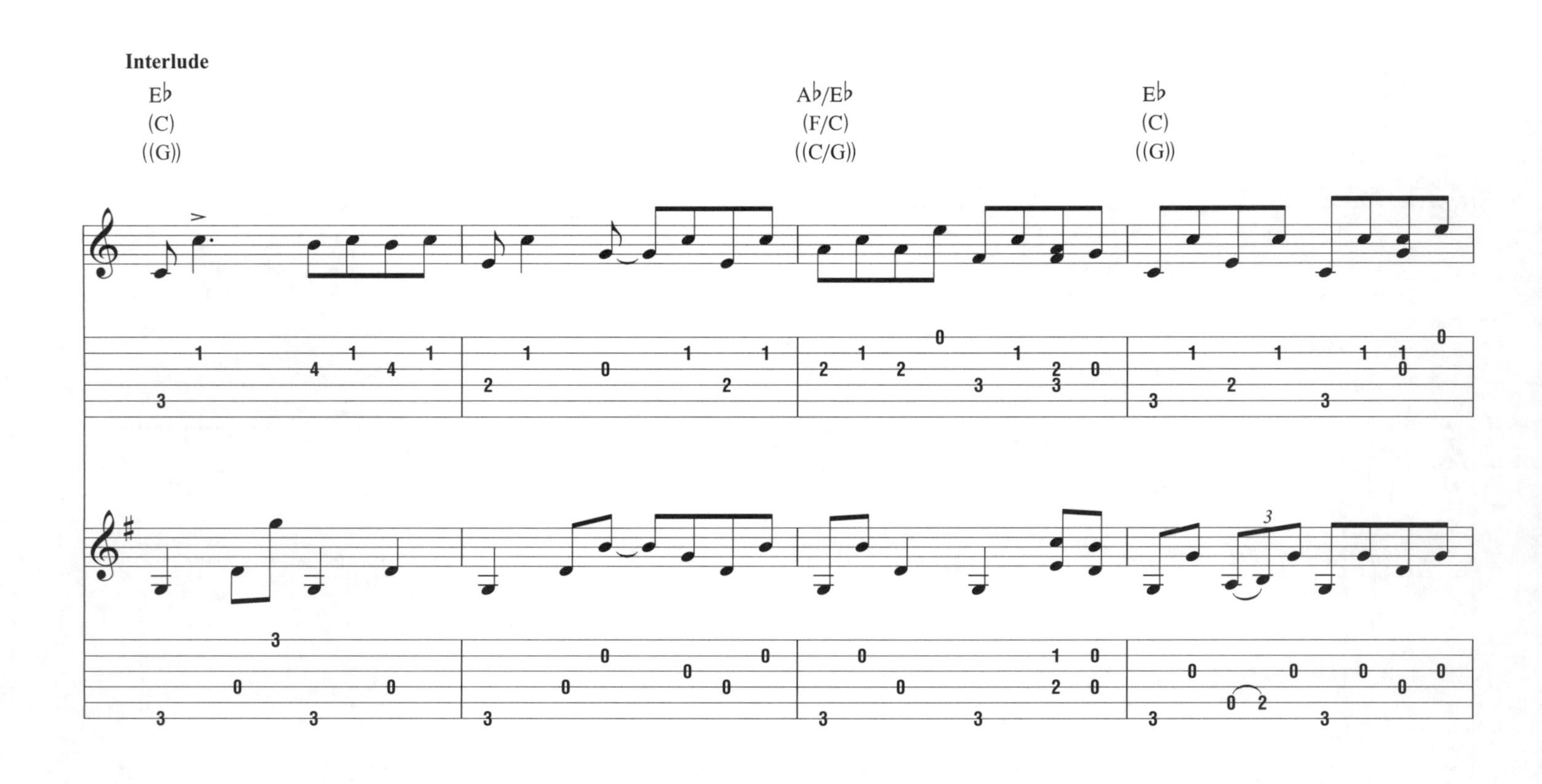
Interlude
E♭
(C)
((G))
A♭/E♭
(F/C)
((C/G))
E♭
(C)
((G))

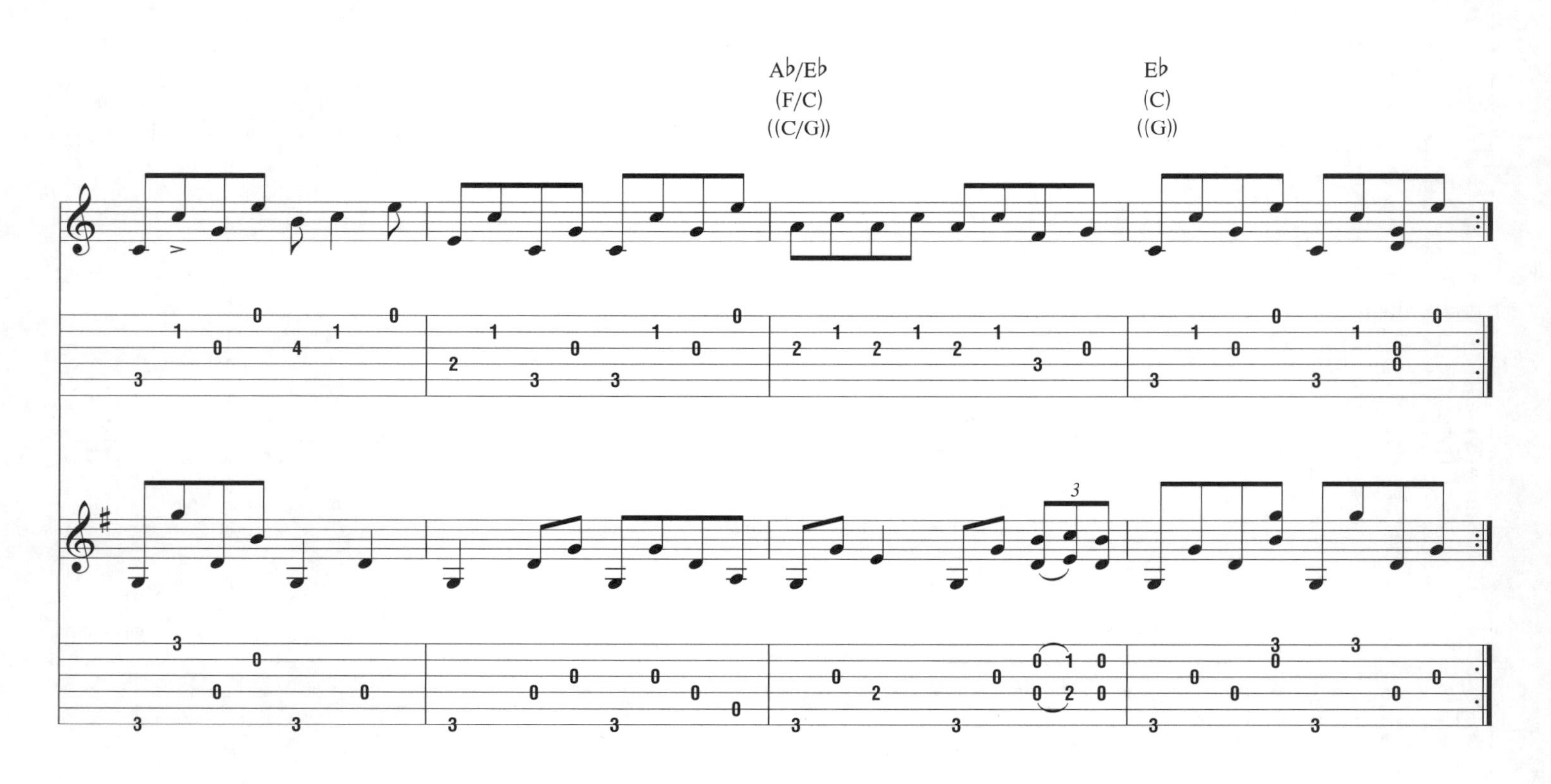
A♭/E♭
(F/C)
((C/G))
E♭
(C)
((G))

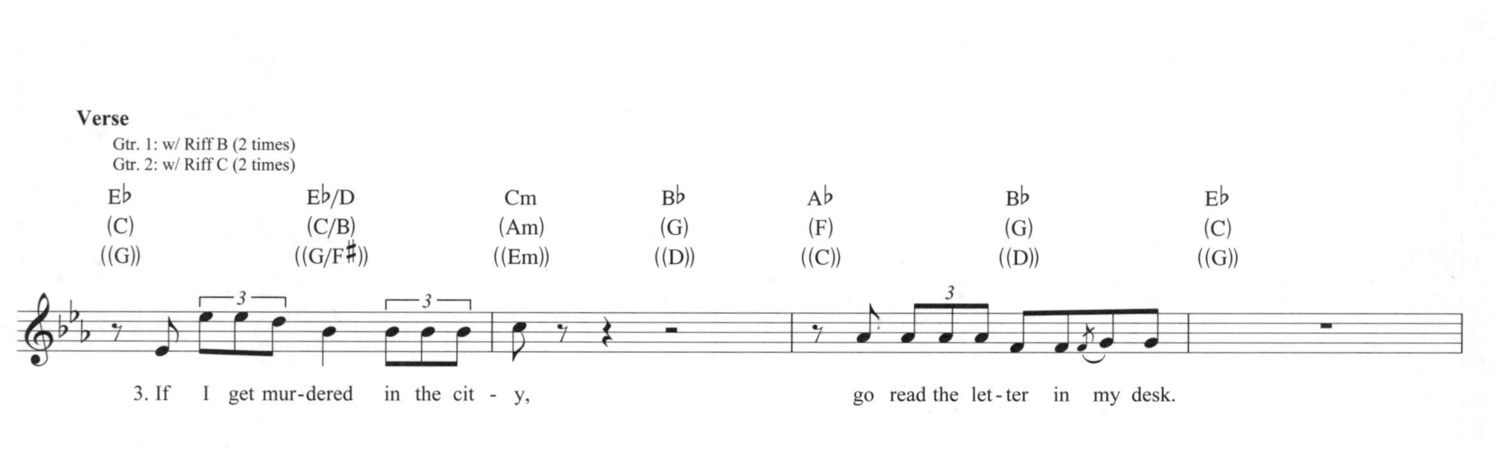
Verse
Gtr. 1: w/ Riff B (2 times)
Gtr. 2: w/ Riff C (2 times)
E♭
(C)
((G))
E♭/D
(C/B)
((G/F♯))
Cm
(Am)
((Em))
B♭
(G)
((D))
A♭
(F)
((C))
B♭
(G)
((D))
E♭
(C)
((G))
3. If I get mur-dered in the cit - y,
go read the let-ter in my desk.

Eb/D (C/B) ((G/F#)) Cm (Am) ((Em)) Bb (G) ((D)) Ab (F) ((C)) Bb (G) ((D)) Eb (C) ((G))
Don't both-er with all my be-long - ings, but pay at - ten-tion to the list.
Gtrs. 1 & 2: w/ Riffs D & D1
Cm (Am) ((Em)) Bb (G) ((D)) Eb (C) ((G)) Cm (Am) ((Em)) Bb (G) ((D)) Eb (C) ((G))
Make sure my sis-ter knows I loved her. Make sure my moth-er knows the same.
Cm (Am) ((Em)) Bb (G) ((D)) Ab (F) ((C)) Eb (C) ((G)) Bb5 (G5) ((D5))
Al - ways re - mem - ber there was noth - ing worth shar - ing like the love that let us share our name.
Eb (C) ((G)) Cm (Am) ((Em)) Bb (G) ((D)) Ab (F) ((C)) Eb (C) ((G))
Al - ways re - mem - ber there was noth - ing worth shar - ing like the
Gtr. 1
Gtr. 2

Outro
B♭
(G)
((D))
E♭
(C)
((G))
love that let us share our name.
A♭/E♭
(F/C)
((C/G))
E♭
(C)
((G))
A♭/E♭
(F/C)
((C/G))
E♭
(C)
((G))
rit.
rit.

from *Emotionalism*

Paranoia in B Flat Major

Words and Music by Scott Avett, Seth Avett and Robert Crawford

Capo III

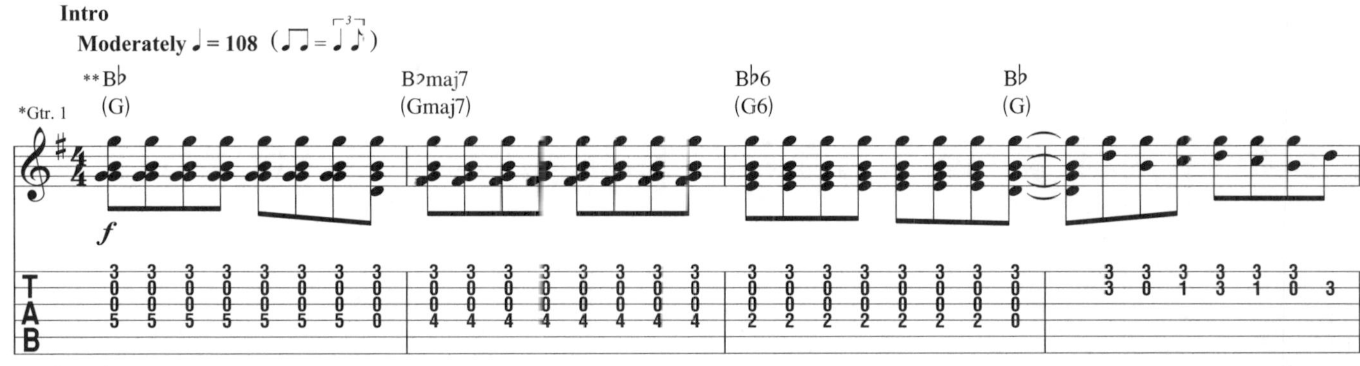

*Banjo arr. for gtr.

**Symbols in parentheses represent chord names respective to capoed guitar. Symbols above represent actual sounding chords. Capoed fret is "0" in tab. Chord symbols reflect overall harmony.

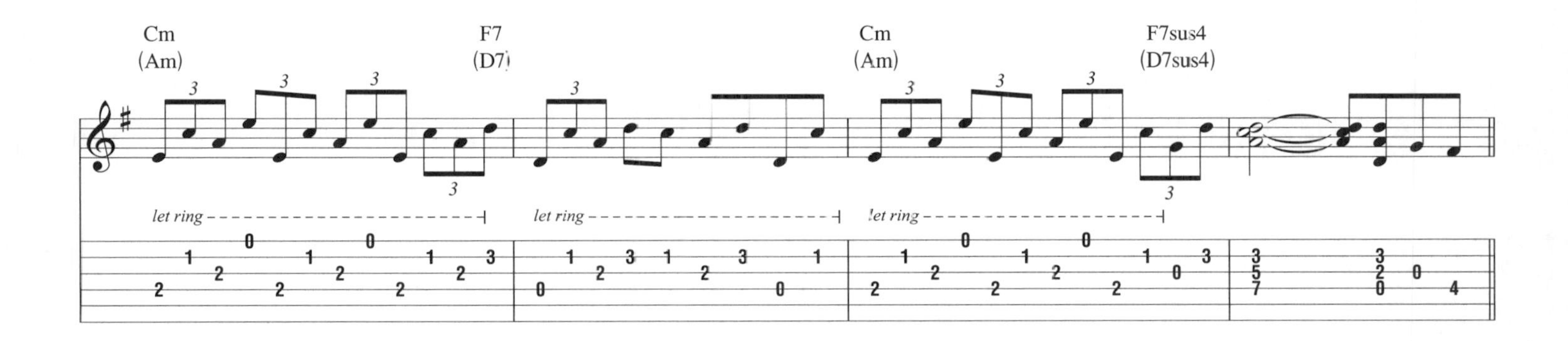

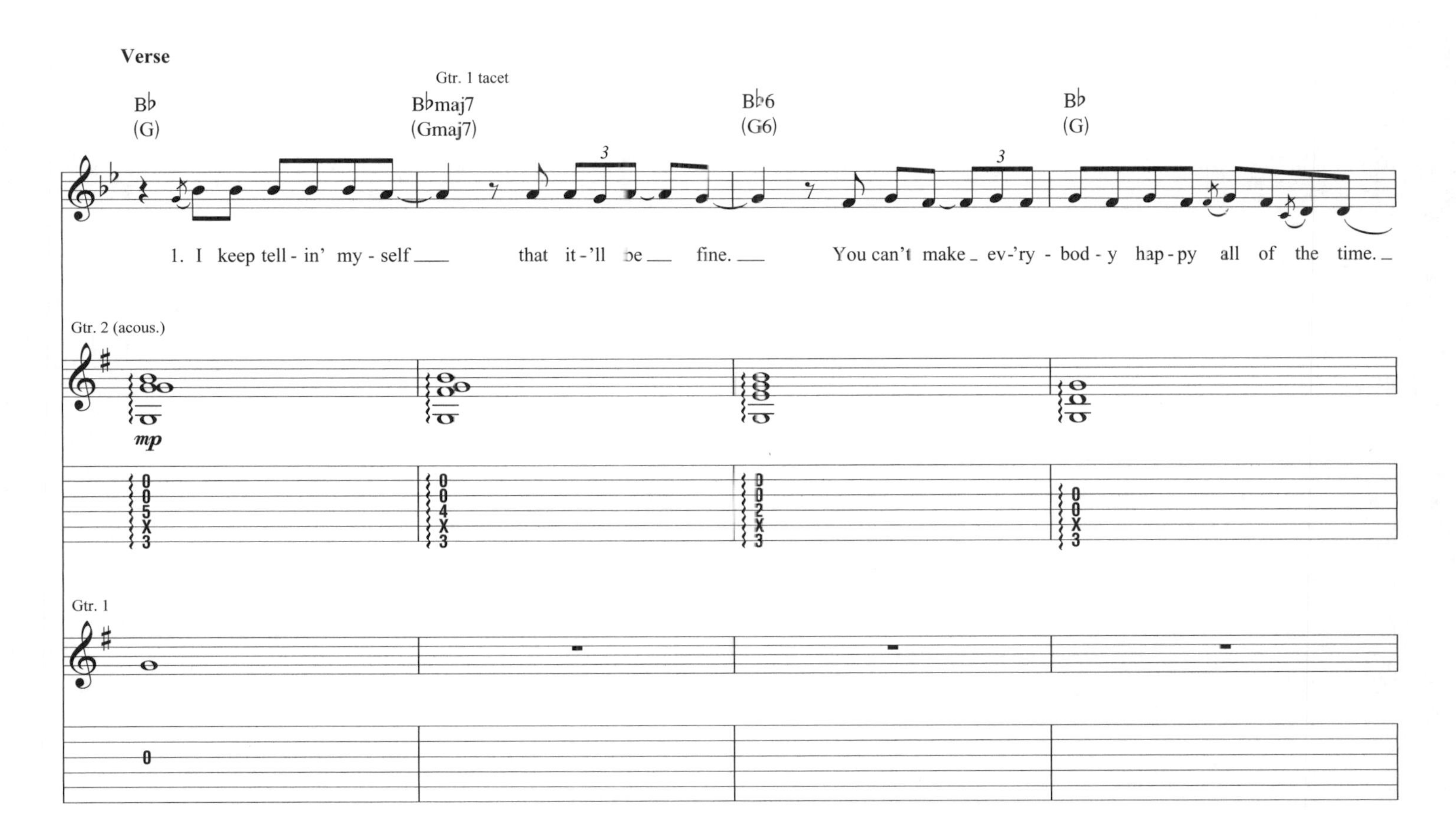

Cm (Am)
F7 (D7)
B♭ (G)
B♭maj7 (Gmaj7)
But I have found my - self in a place that I've nev - er been,
Gtr. 2
let ring
B♭6 (G6)
B♭ (G)
Cm (Am)
F7 (D7)
a place that I thought that I would nev-er be,
those peo-ple look - in' back at me.
let ring
Verse
B♭ (G)
B♭ (G)
B♭maj7 (Gmaj7)
2. I keep hav - in' this dream, I'm at a par - ty,
Rhy. Fig. 1
w/ pick & finger
let ring
w/ pick
*Tap lower bout of guitar with palm of pick-hand.
B♭6 (G6)
B♭ (G)
Cm (Am)
F7 (D7)
there's peo-ple throw-in' drinks and scream-in', tell - in' me that I don't be-long.
End Rhy. Fig. 1

Gtr. 2: w/ Rhy. Fig. 1 (1st 4 meas.)
B♭ (G)
B♭maj7 (Gmaj7)
B♭6 (G6)
B♭ (G)
Late-ly life's been the same, I find this comf-'ter - ble place with all my friends and then my friends start tell-in' me that I've
Cm (Am)
F7 (D7)
B♭ (G)
al - ways been wrong.
(I'm so tired of be-in' wrong.)
Gtr. 2
let ring
Interlude
B♭ (G)
B♭add9 (Gadd9)
B♭ (G)
B♭maj7 (Gmaj7)
E♭maj7 (Cmaj7)
let ring
E♭6 (C6)
Gm (Em)
F (D)
let ring
Verse
Gtr. 2: w/ Rhy. Fig. 1 (2 times)
B♭ (G)
B♭maj7 (Gmaj7)
B♭6 (G5)
B♭ (G)
3. There was a time I could move, there was a time I could breathe. The crowd-ed spac-es filled with an-gry fac-es, it did-n't once
Cm (Am)
F7 (D7)
B♭ (G)
B♭maj7 (Gmaj7)
cross my mind.
With par - a - noi - a in my heels, will you love me still,

Bb6
(G6)
Bb
(G)
Cm
(Am)
F7
(D7)
when we a - wake and you find that the san - i - ty is gone from my eyes?
(Yeah.)
Interlude
Bb
(G)
Cm
(Am)
Dm
(Bm)
Eb
(C)
Bb
(G)
Dm
(Bm)
Gtr. 2
*As before
Cm
(Am)
Bb
(G)
Cm
(Am)
Dm
(Bm)
Eb
(C)
Bb
(G)
(Yeah.)
let ring
**As before
Verse
Gtr. 2: w/ Rhy. Fig. 1 (1st 4 meas.)
Bb
(G)
Bbmaj7
(Gmaj7)
Bb6
(G6)
Bb
(G)
4. I got se - crets from you, you got se - crets from me, be - cause you're so wor - ried a - bout what I'm gon - na
Cm
(Am)
F7
(D7)
Bb
(G)
think.
Ba - by, I'm wor - ried too.
Gtr. 2
let ring

Gtr. 2: w/ Rhy. Fig. 1 (1st 4 meas.)
B♭maj7
(Gmaj7)
B♭6
(G6)
B♭
(G)
But if love is a game, girl, then you're gon-na win. I'll spend the rest of my life bring in' vic-to-ry

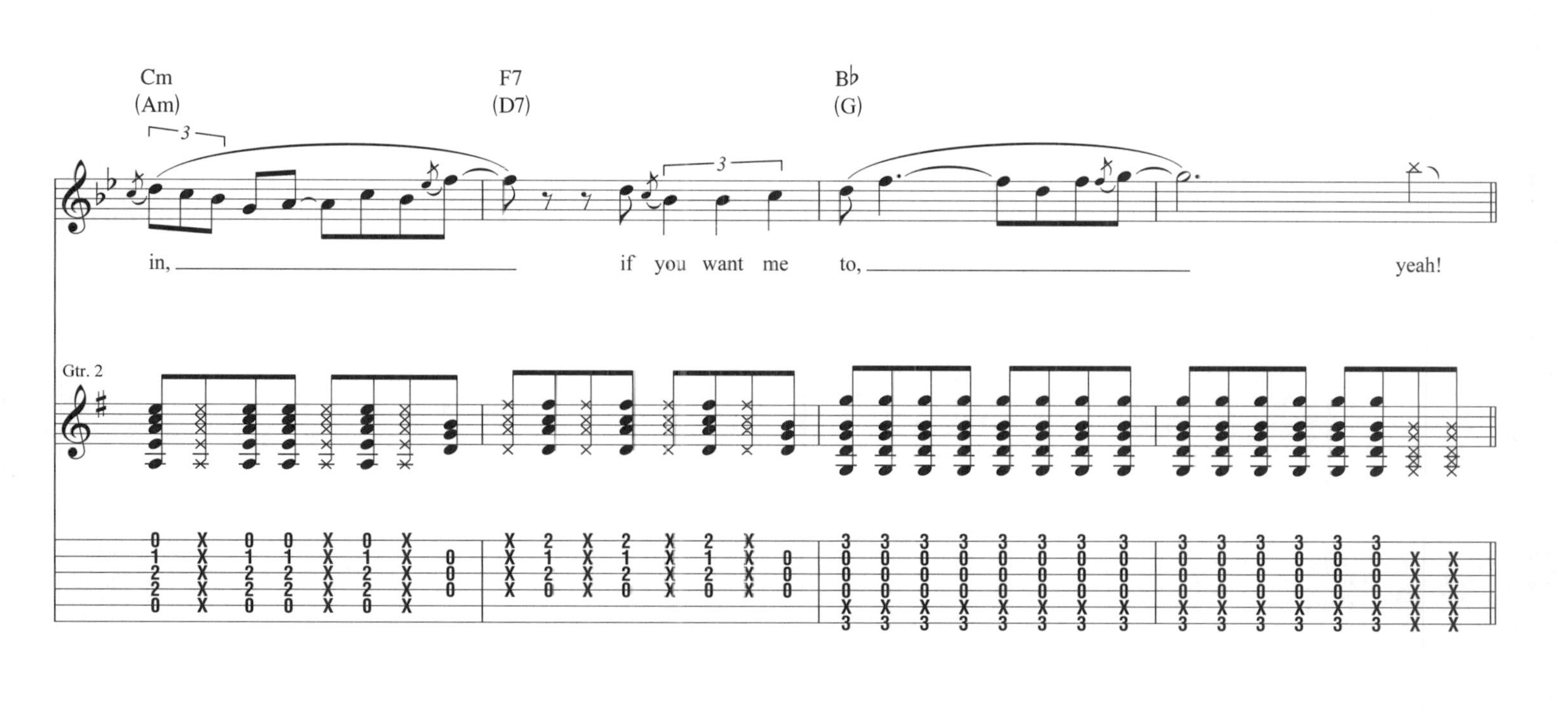
Cm
(Am)
F7
(D7)
B♭
(G)
in, if you want me to, yeah!
Gtr. 2

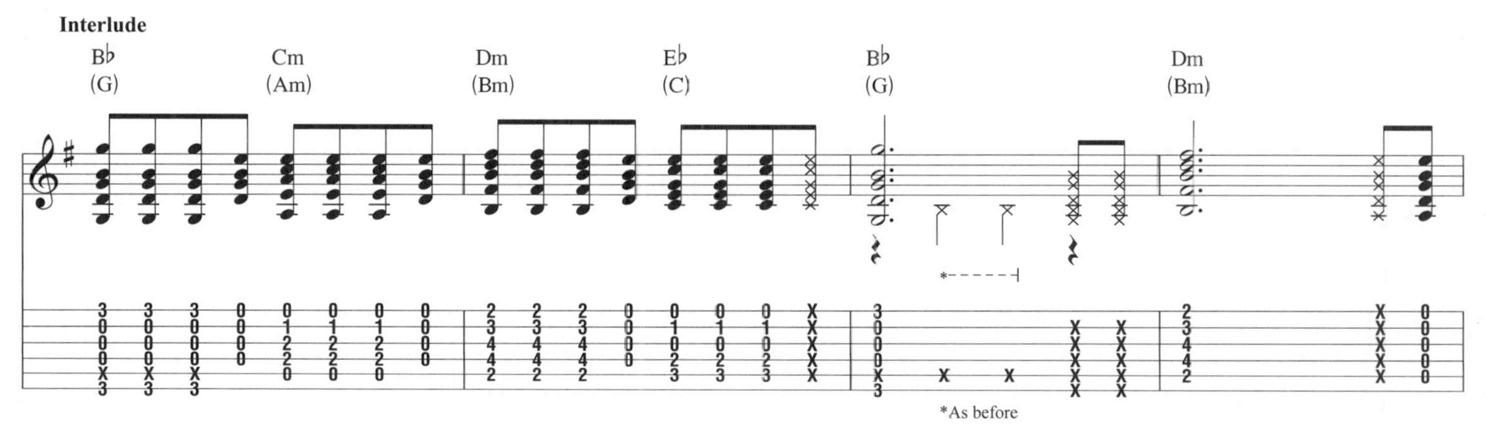
Interlude
B♭
(G)
Cm
(Am)
Dm
(Bm)
E♭
(C)
B♭
(G)
Dm
(Bm)
*As before

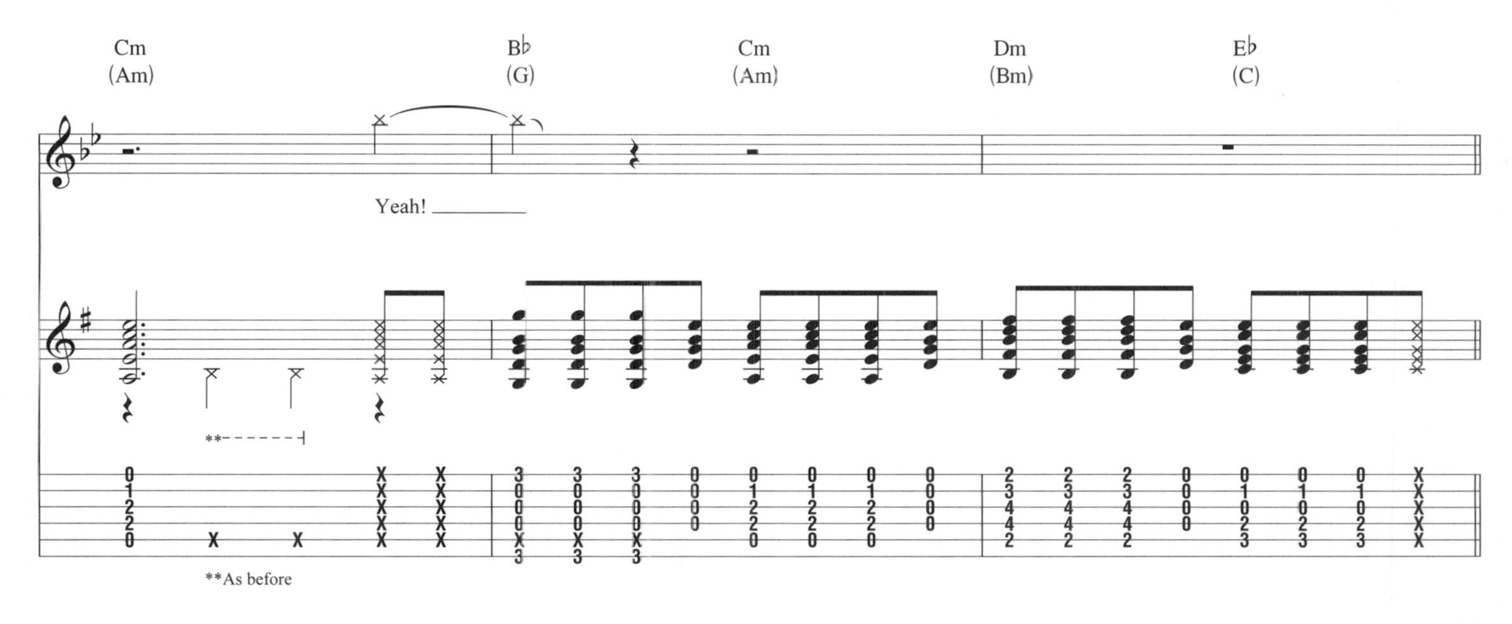
Cm
(Am)
B♭
(G)
Cm
(Am)
Dm
(Bm)
E♭
(C)
Yeah!
**As before

Outro
B♭ (G)
B♭add9 (Gadd9)
B♭ (G)
B♭maj7 (Gmaj7)
(La, la, la, la, da, la, da, da, da.
(La, la, la, la, da, ah, da.
w/ fingers
let ring
E♭maj9 (Cmaj9)
Gm (Em)
F7 (D7)
La, da, la, da, la, da.
La, la, da, la, da, la, da.
let ring
B♭ (G)
B♭maj7 (Gmaj7)
B♭6 (G6)
B♭ (G)
La, da, la, da, la, da.
La, la, da, la, da, la, da.
E♭ (C)
Gm (Em)
F7 (D7)
B♭ (G)
poco rit.
La, da, la, da, la, da. Ah.)
La, la, da, la, da, la, da.)

from *Emotionalism*

Shame

Words and Music by Scott Avett, Seth Avett and Robert Crawford

Capo I

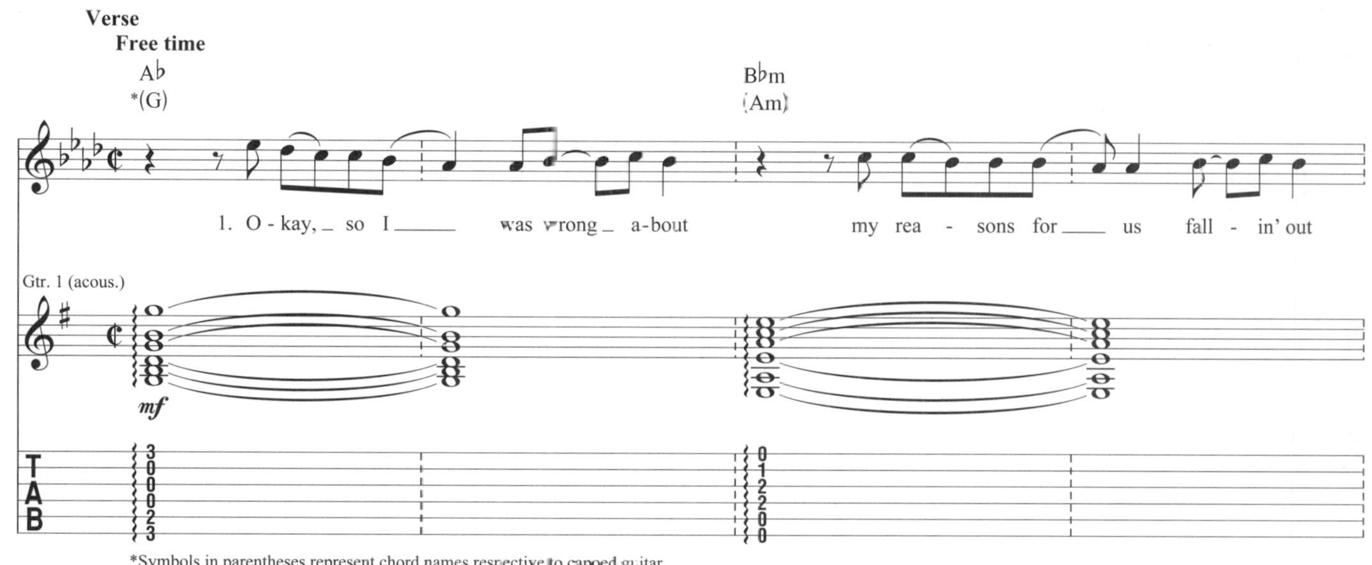

*Symbols in parentheses represent chord names respective to capoed guitar. Symbols above reflect actual sounding chords. Capoed fret is "0" in tab.

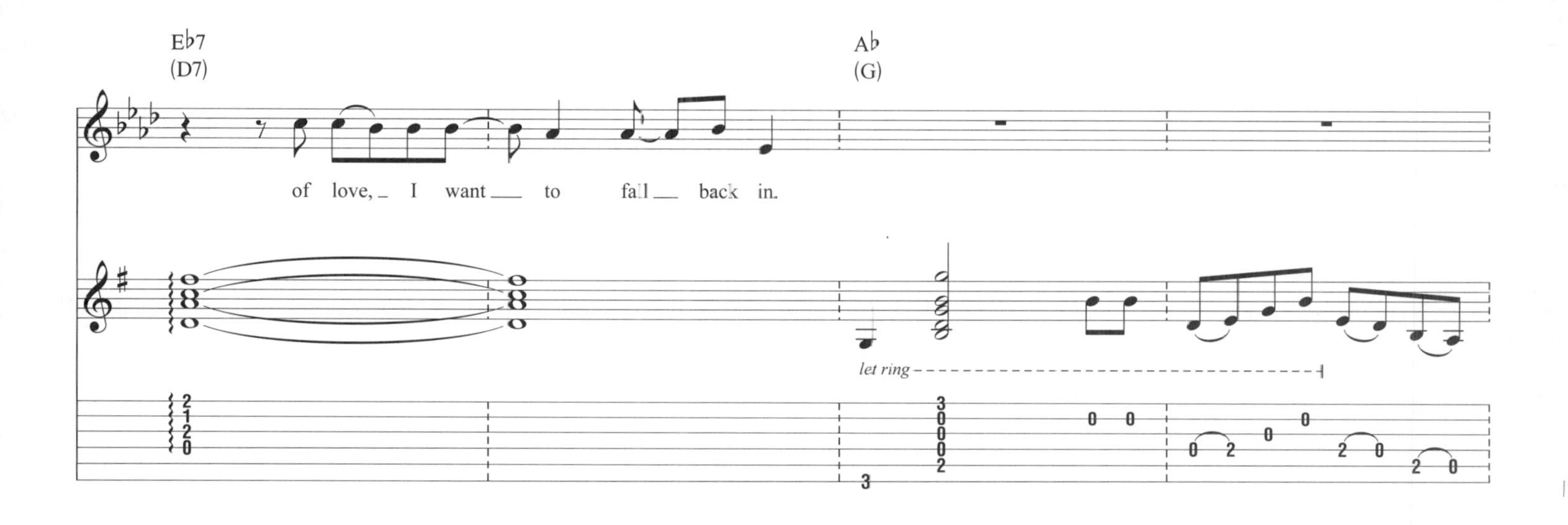

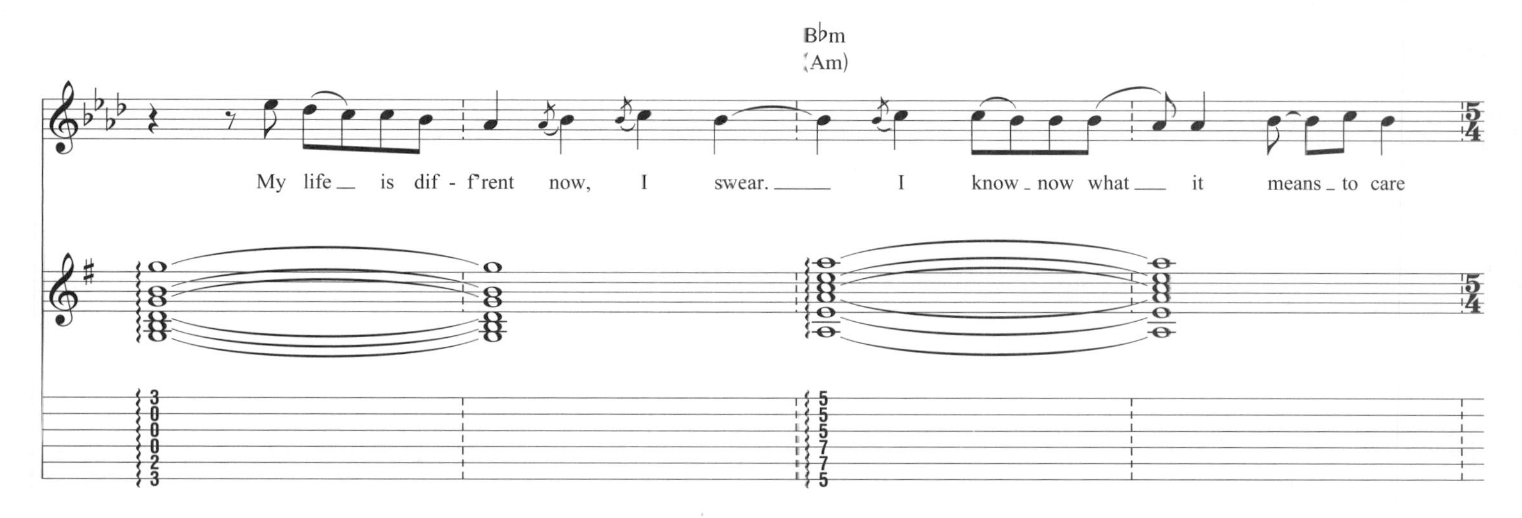

E♭7
(D7)
A♭
(G)
a - bout some - bod - y oth - er than my - self.
Harm.
let ring
B♭m
(Am)
I know the things I said to you, they were un - ten - der and un - true.
Rhy. Fig. 1
E♭7
(D7)
A♭
(G)
I'd like to see those things un - do.
let ring
End Rhy. Fig. 1
Gtr. 1: w/ Rhy. Fig. 1
B♭m
(Am)
So if you could find it in your heart to give a man a sec - ond start,

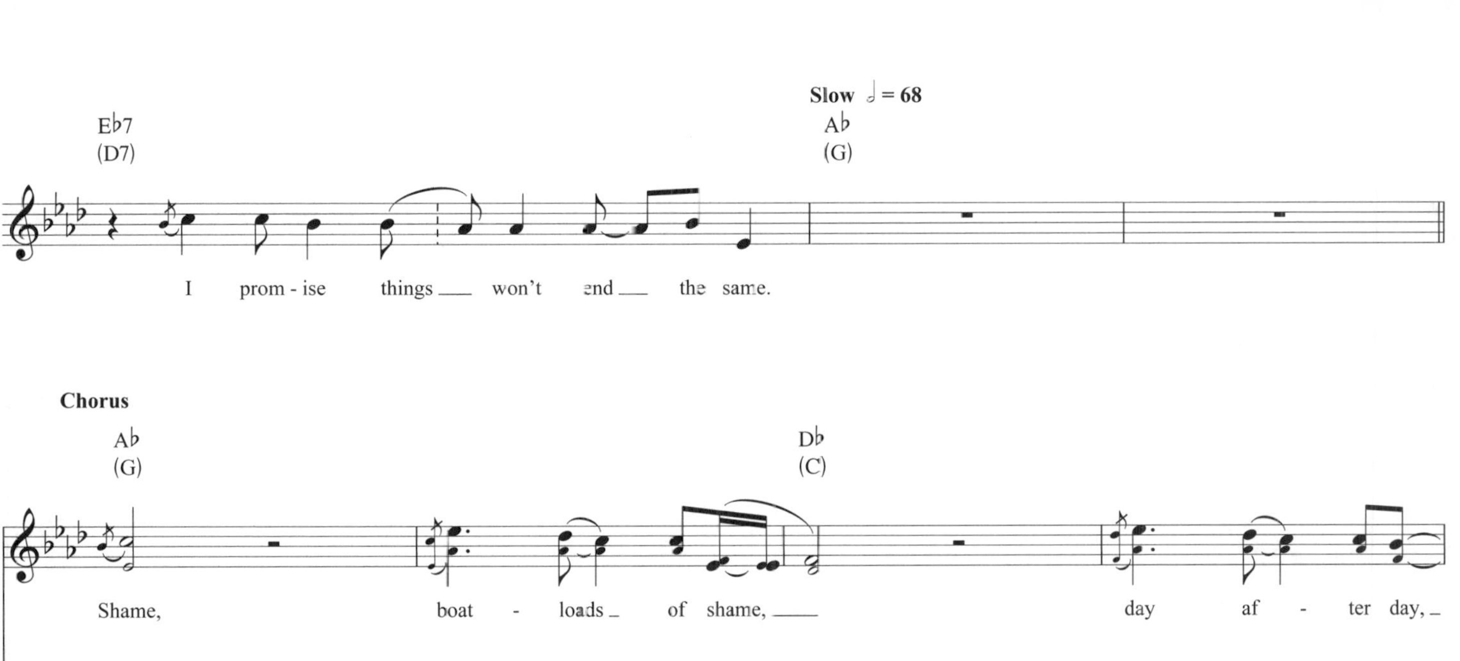
Slow 𝅗𝅥 = 68
Eb7
(D7)
Ab
(G)
I prom - ise things won't end the same.
Chorus
Ab
(G)
Db
(C)
Shame, boat - loads of shame, day af - ter day,

Gtr. 1
Rhy. Fig. 2
Bbm
(Am)
Eb7
(D7)
more of the same.
End Rhy. Fig. 2
let ring

Gtr. 1: w/ Rhy. Fig. 2
Ab
(G)
Db
(C)
Blame,
(Blame,)
please lift it off,
please take it off,

Bbm
(Am)
Eb7
(D7)
please make it stop.

Verse
A♭
(G)
B♭m
(Am)
2. O - kay, so I have read the mail, the sto - ries peo - ple of - ten tell
Gtr. 1
E♭7
(D7)
A♭
(G)
Fm
(Em)
A♭/G
(G/F♯)
a - bout us that we nev - er knew.
let ring
B♭m
(Am)
But their ex - ist - ence will float a - way, and just like ev - 'ry word they say,
let ring
let ring
E♭7
(D7)
A♭
(G)
Fm
(Em)
A♭/G
(G/F♯)
and we will hold hands as they fade.
let ring
let ring

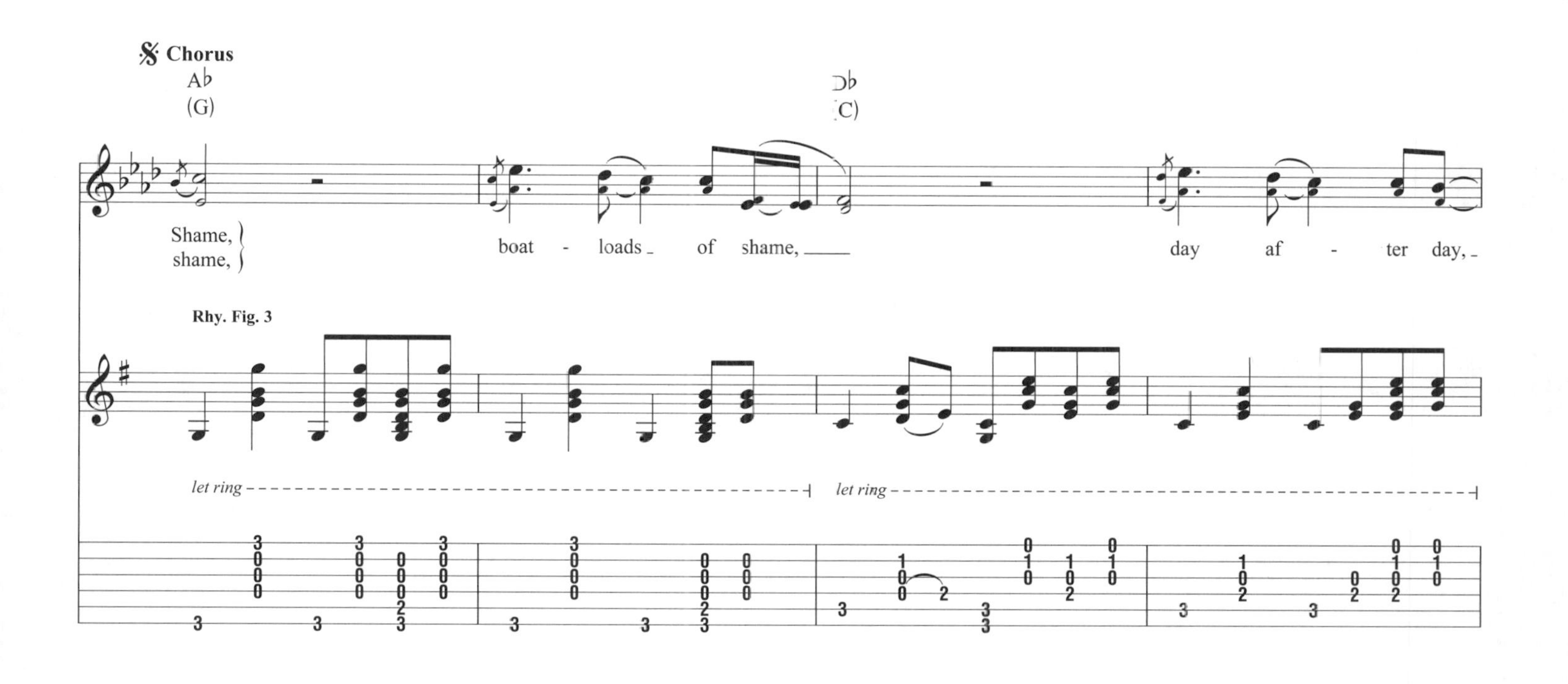
Chorus
A♭
(G)
D♭
(C)
Shame, shame,
boat - loads of shame,
day af - ter day,
Rhy. Fig. 3
let ring
let ring

B♭m
(Am)
E♭7
(D7)
Fm
(Em)
A♭/G
(G/F♯)
more of the same.
End Rhy. Fig. 3
let ring
let ring

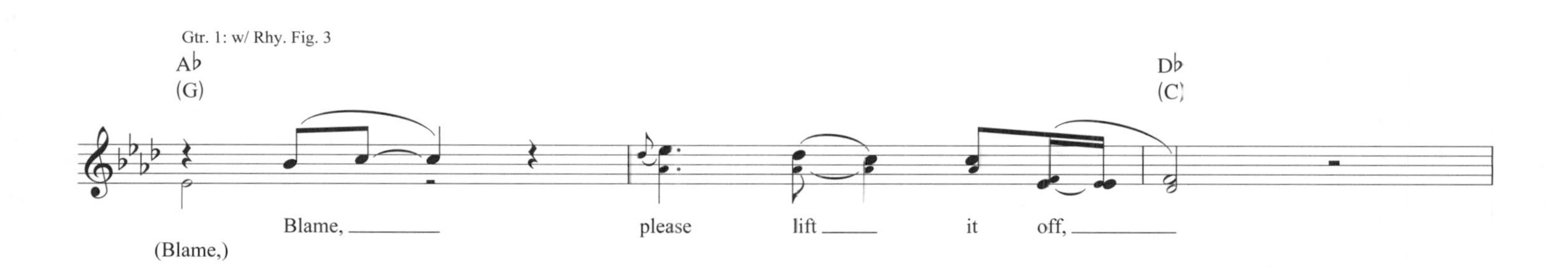
Gtr. 1: w/ Rhy. Fig. 3
A♭
(G)
D♭
(C)
Blame,
(Blame,)
please lift it off,

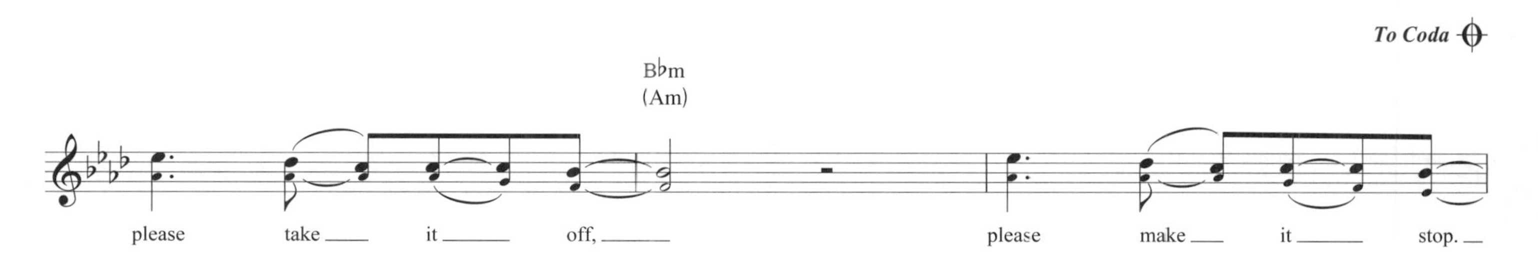
To Coda
B♭m
(Am)
please take it off,
please make it stop.

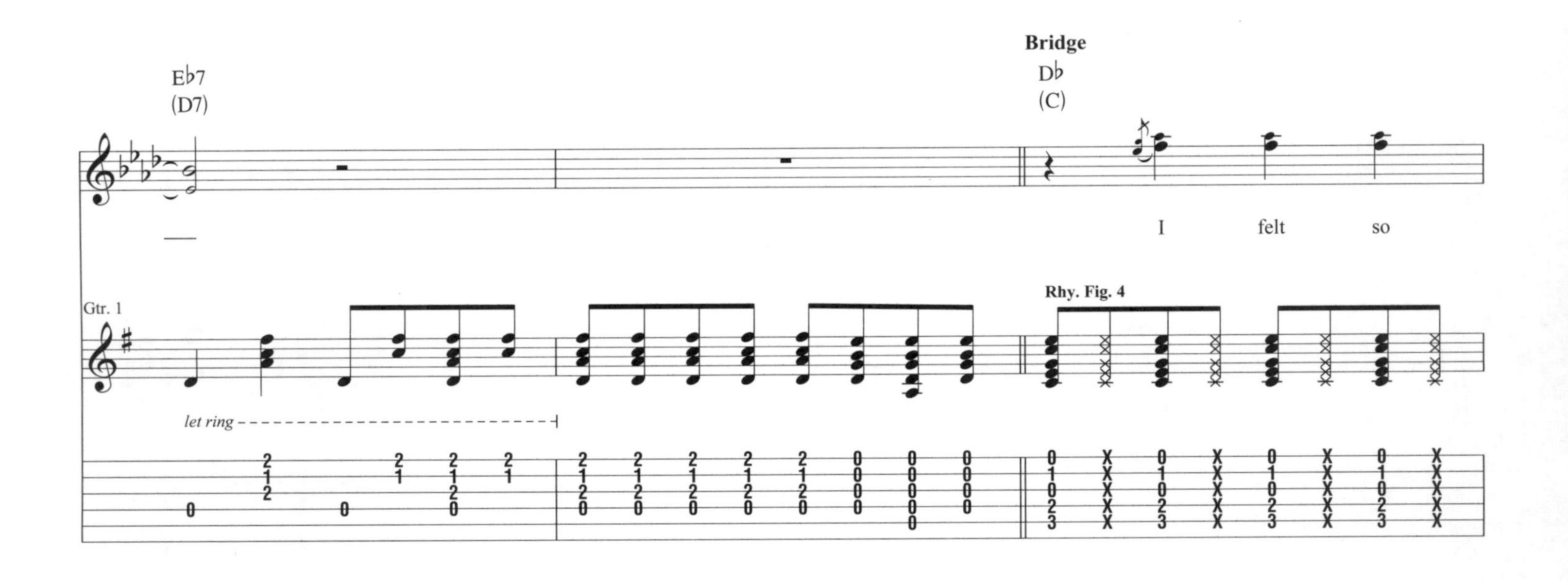

Bridge
E♭7
(D7)
D♭
(C)
I felt so
Gtr. 1
Rhy. Fig. 4
let ring

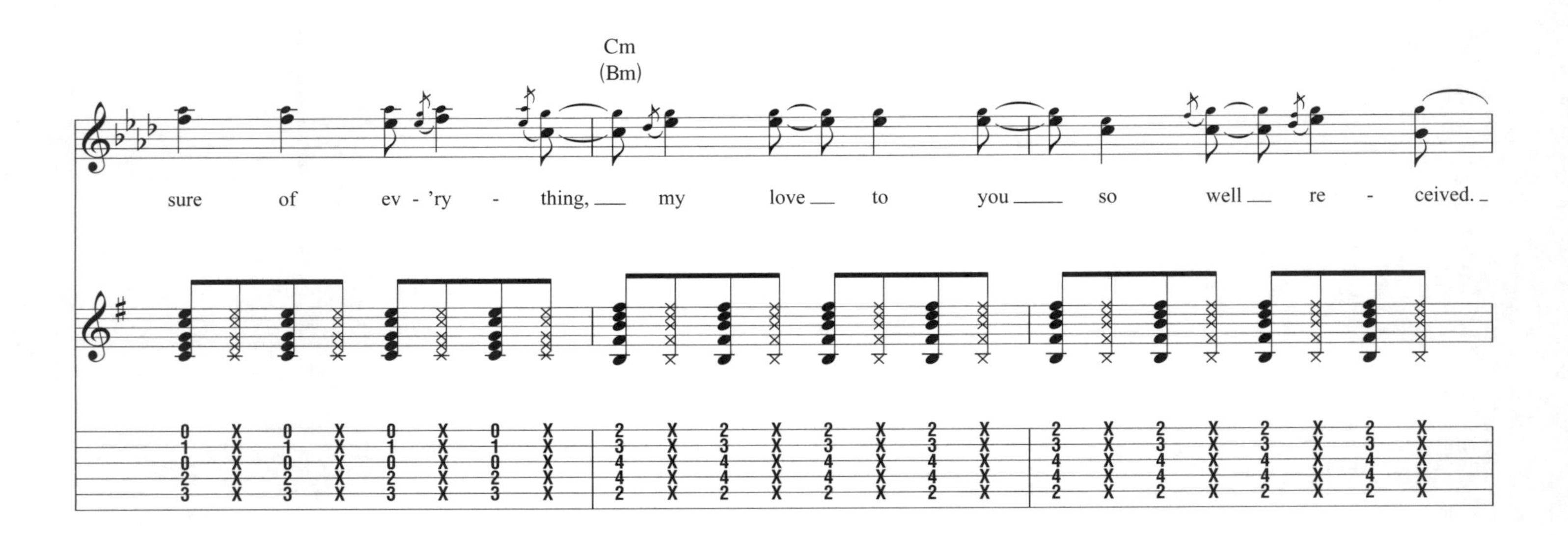

Cm
(Bm)
sure of ev - 'ry - thing, my love to you so well re - ceived.

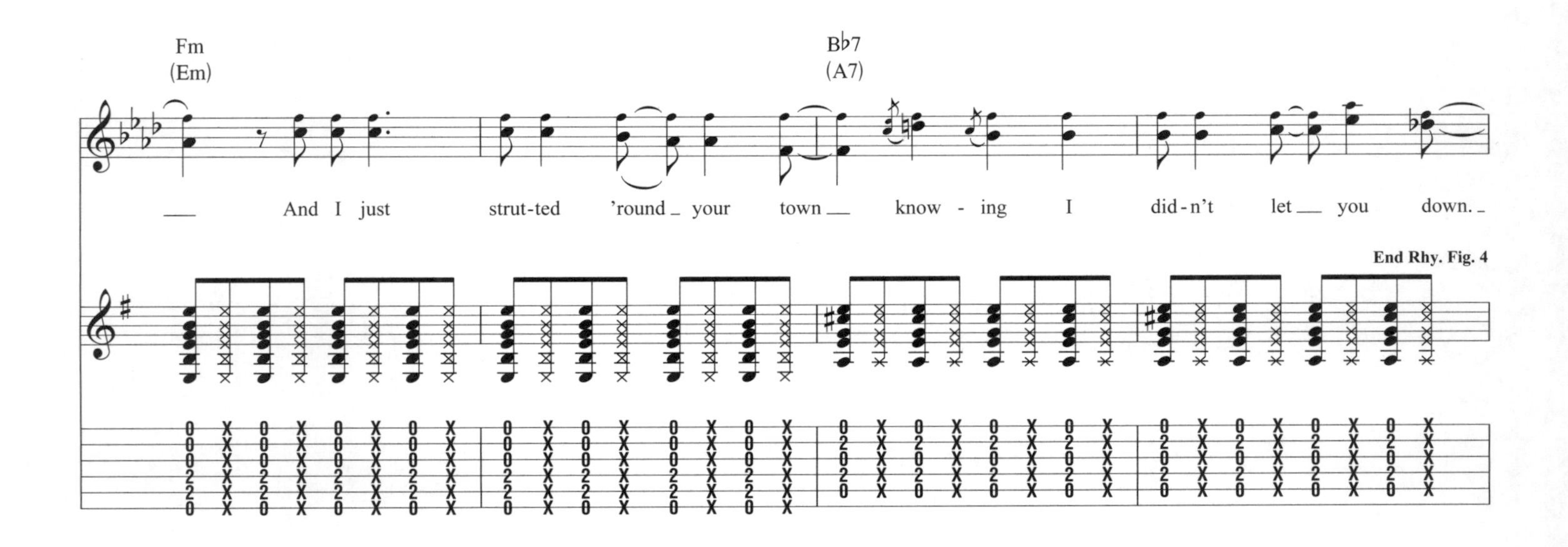

Fm
(Em)
B♭7
(A7)
And I just strut-ted 'round your town know - ing I did-n't let you down.
End Rhy. Fig. 4

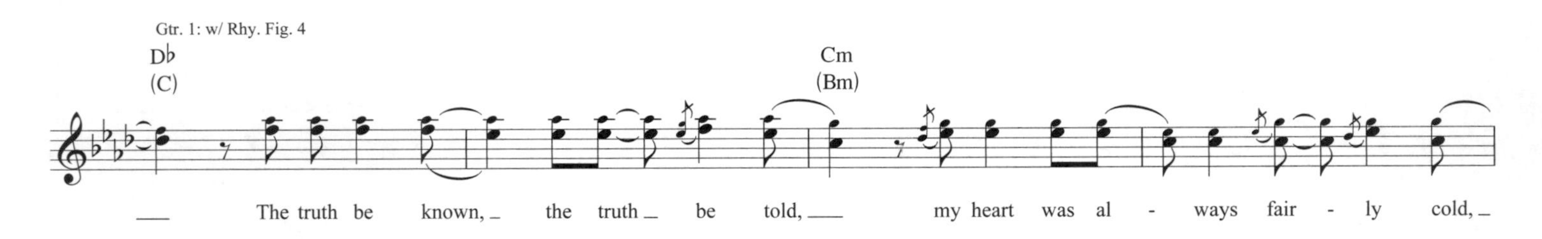

Gtr. 1: w/ Rhy. Fig. 4
D♭
(C)
Cm
(Bm)
The truth be known, the truth be told, my heart was al - ways fair - ly cold,

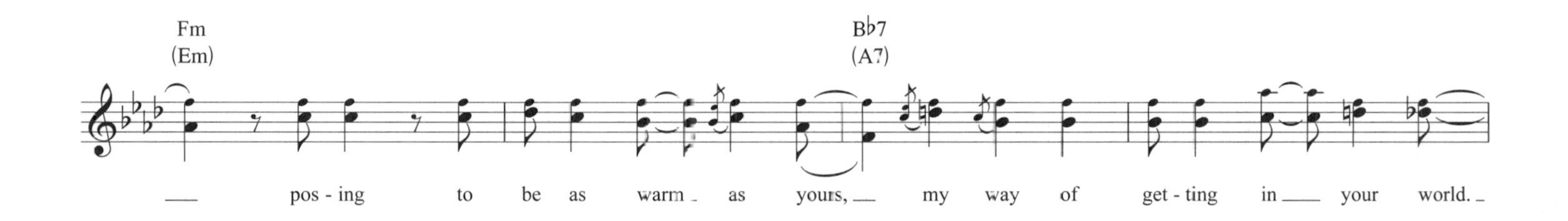
Fm
(Em)
B♭7
(A7)
pos - ing to be as warm as yours, my way of get - ting in your world.

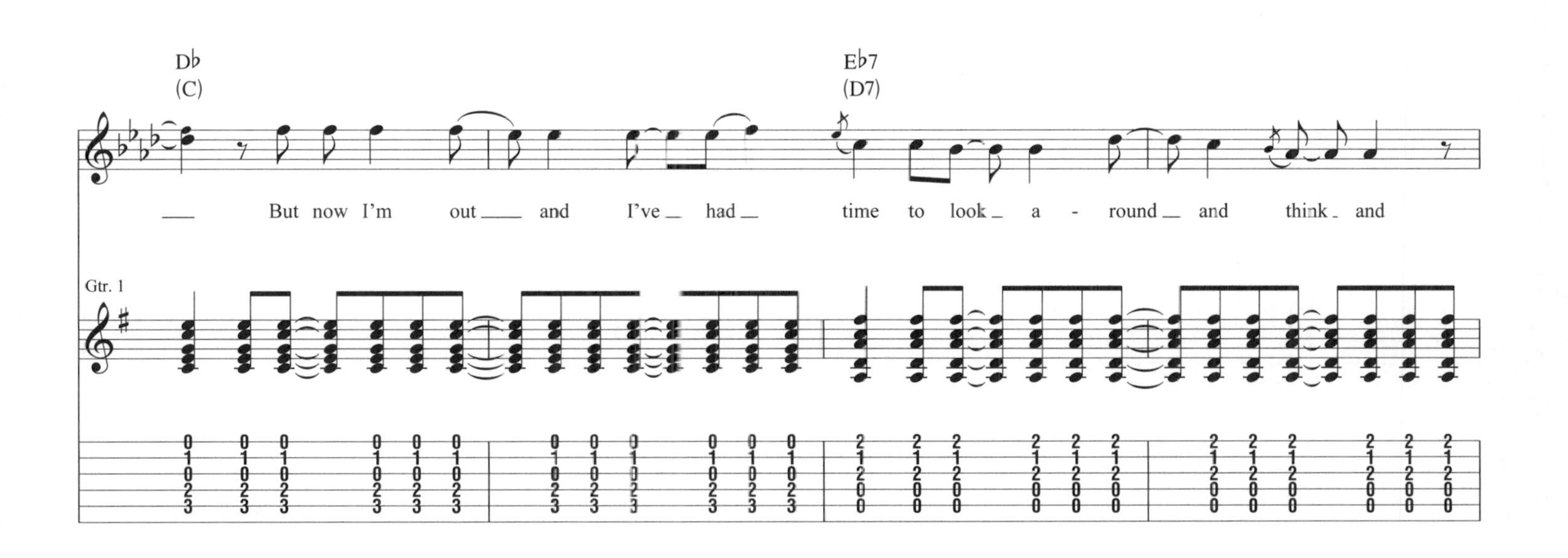
D♭
(C)
E♭7
(D7)
But now I'm out and I've had time to look a - round and think and
Gtr. 1

D♭
(C)
E♭7
(D7)
see in - to an - oth - er world that's filled with guilt and o -

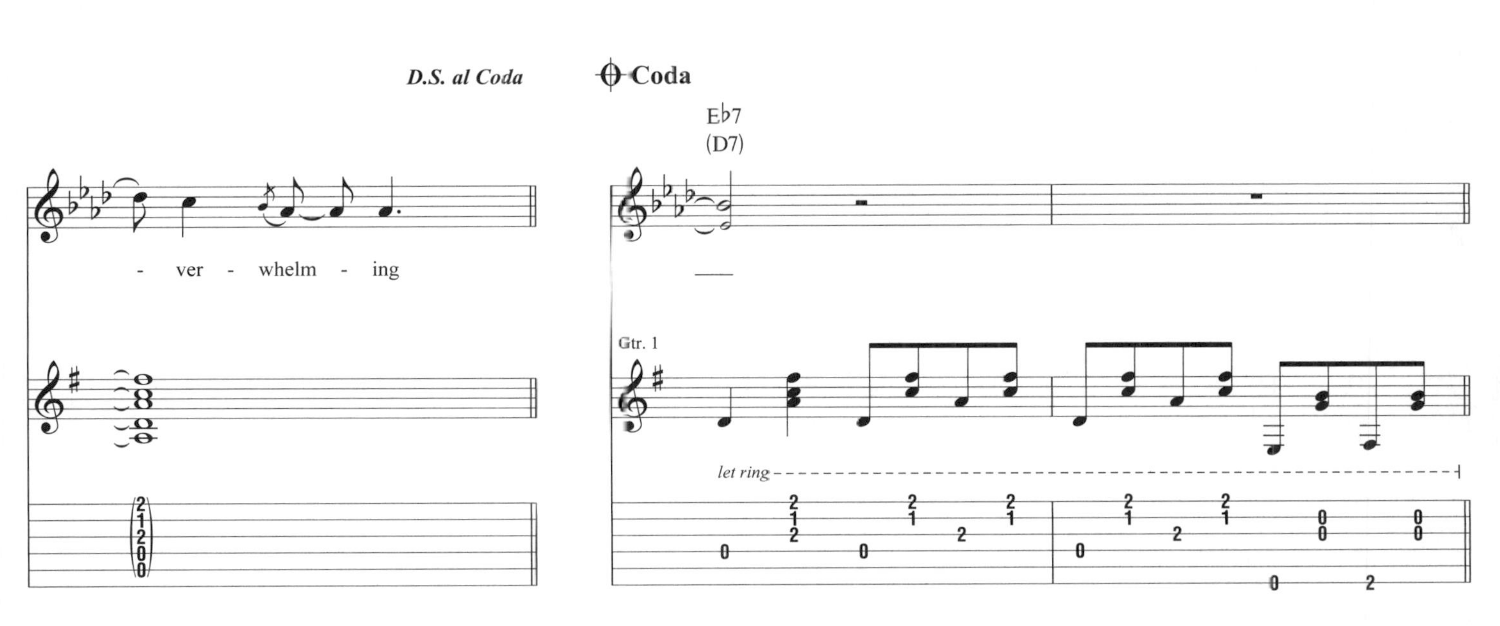
D.S. al Coda
Coda
E♭7
(D7)
- ver - whelm - ing
Gtr. 1
let ring

Outro-Verse
A♭5
(G5)
B♭m
(Am)
3. And ev - 'ry - one, they have a heart, and when they break and fall a - part,
E♭7
(D7)
A♭
(G)
they need some - bod - y's help - in' hand.
let ring
Fm
(Em)
A♭
(G)
B♭m
(Am)
I used to say, "Just let 'em fall," it would - n't both -
let ring
E♭7
(D7)
N.C.
rit.
- er me at all. I could - n't help then, now I can.
rit.

from *The Second Gleam*

Soul Like the Wheels

Words and Music by Scott Avett, Timothy Avett and Robert Crawford

Open C tuning, capo IV
(low to high) C-G-C-G-C-E

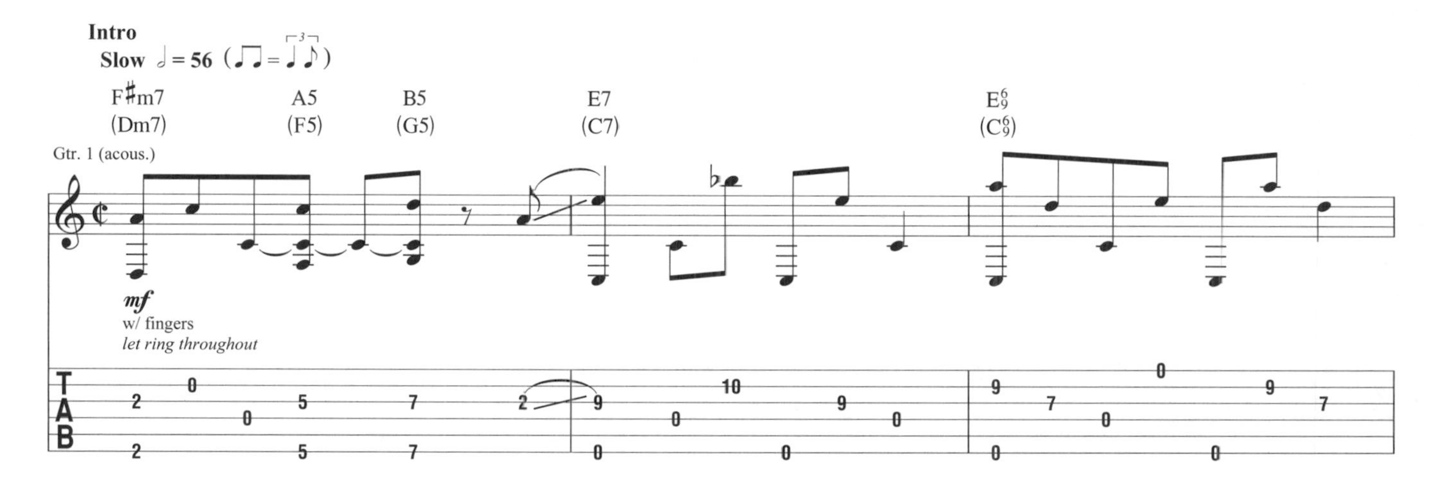

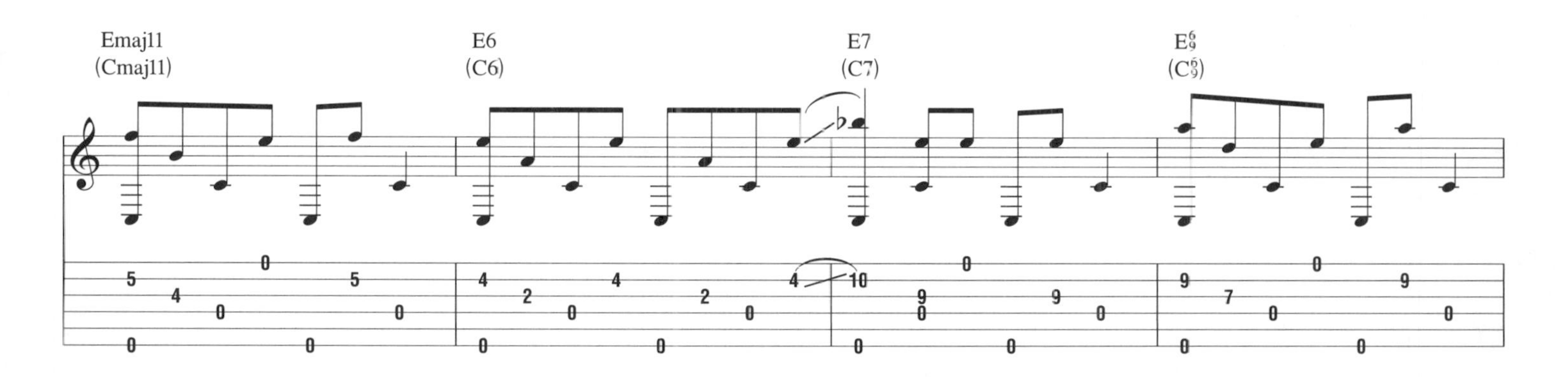

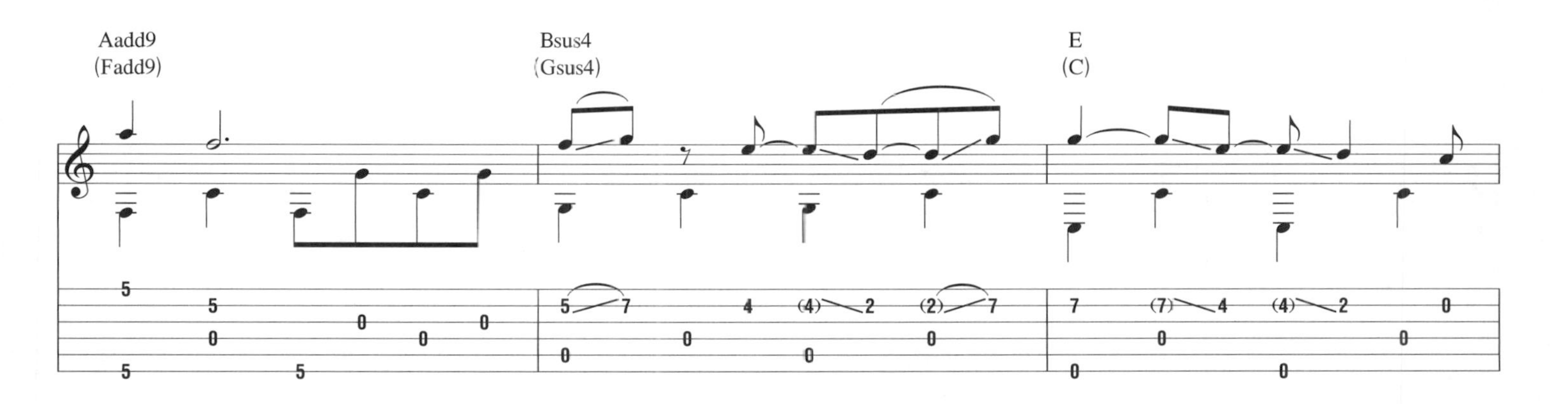

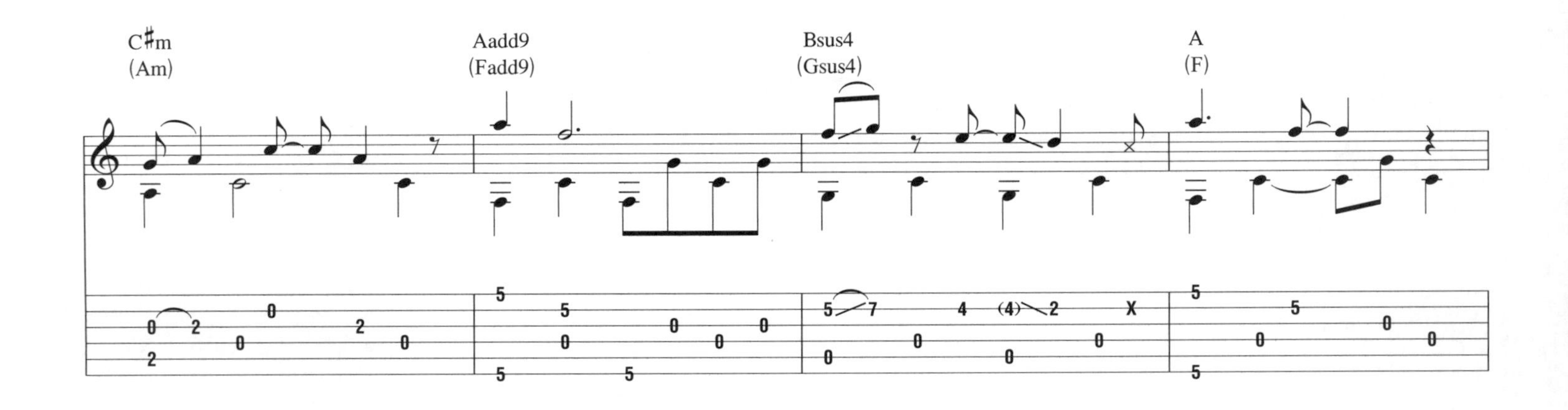
C♯m
(Am)
Aadd9
(Fadd9)
Bsus4
(Gsus4)
A
(F)

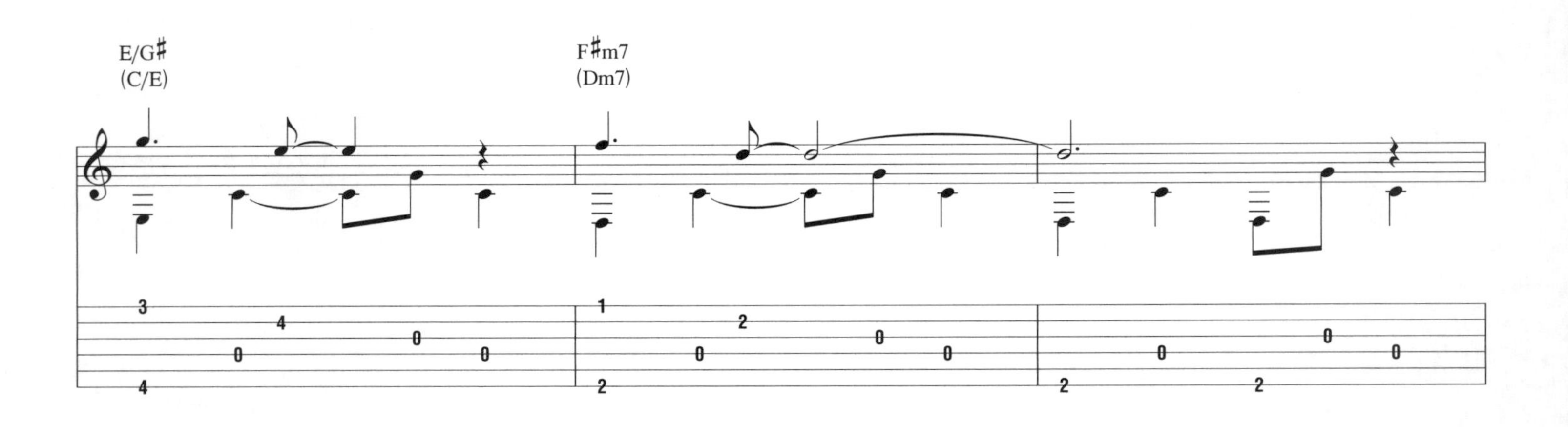
E/G♯
(C/E)
F♯m7
(Dm7)

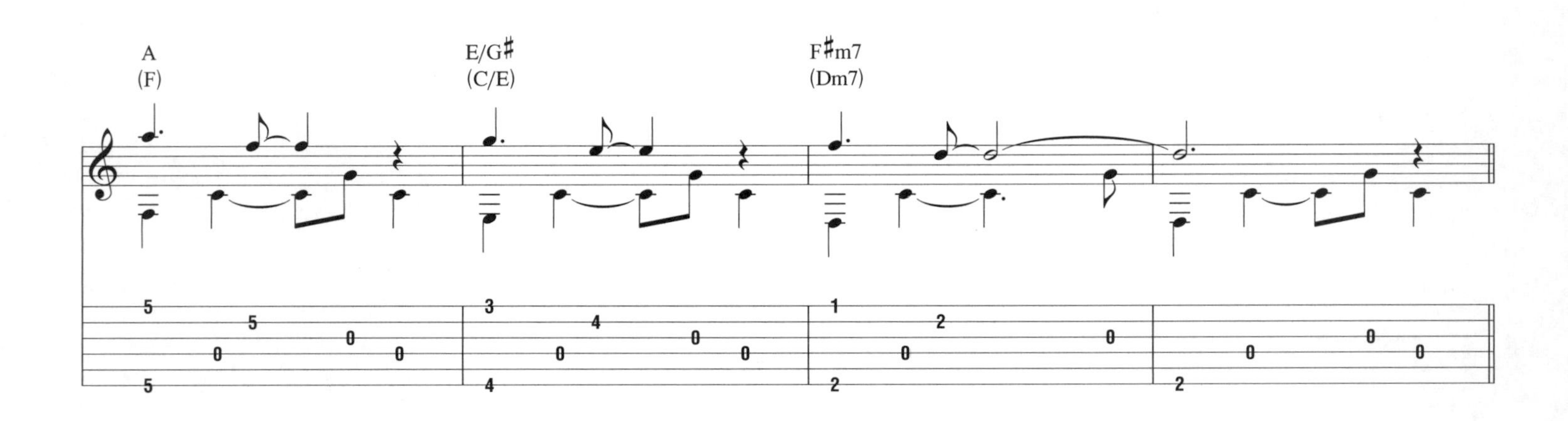
A
(F)
E/G♯
(C/E)
F♯m7
(Dm7)

Verse
E
(C)
C♯m
(Am)
Aadd9
(Fadd9)
Bsus4
(Gsus4)
1. Souls like the wheels, turn - ing, tak - ing us with
2. One lit - tle song, give me strength to leave the
Riff A

E
(C)
C♯m
(Am)
Aadd9
(Fadd9)
Bsus4
(Gsus4)
wind at our heels. Burn - ing, mak - ing us de -
sad and the wrong bur - ied safe - ly in the
End Riff A
Aadd9
(Fadd9)
E/G♯
(C/E)
F♯m
(Dm)
cide on what we're giv - ing.
past where I've been liv - ing.
Riff B
A
(F)
E/G♯
(C/E)
Change this way of
A - live but un - for -
1.
2.
F♯m
(Dm)
liv - ing.
giv - ing.
Let me go,
End Riff B

Chorus
E
(C)
Bsus4/D♯
(Gsus4/B)
C♯m
(Am)
F♯m7
(Dm7)
A5
(F5)
E
(C)
let me go.
Let me go,
let me go.
Interlude
E
(C)
C♯m
(Am)
Aadd9
(Fadd9)
B
(G)
Verse
Gtr. 1: w/ Riff A
E
(C)
C♯m
(Am)
Aadd9
(Fadd9)
Bsus4
(Gsus4)
3. One little girl, bring me light from where I
4. Souls like the wings, spread - ing out a - way from bad
E
(C)
C♯m
(Am)
Aadd9
(Fadd9)
Bsus4
(Gsus4)
thought it was dark. Be the spark that has a
mem - o - ries, make us ca - pa - ble of
Gtr. 1: w/ Riff B
Aadd9
(Fadd9)
E/G♯
(C/E)
F♯m
(Dm)
chance to light the can - dle.
tak - ing off and land - ing.
A -

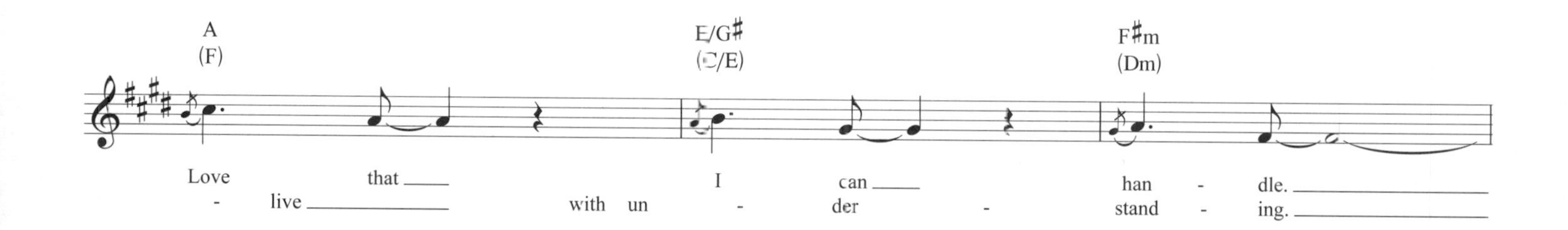
A
(F)
E/G♯
(C/E)
F♯m
(Dm)
Love that I can handle.
- live with un - der - stand - ing.

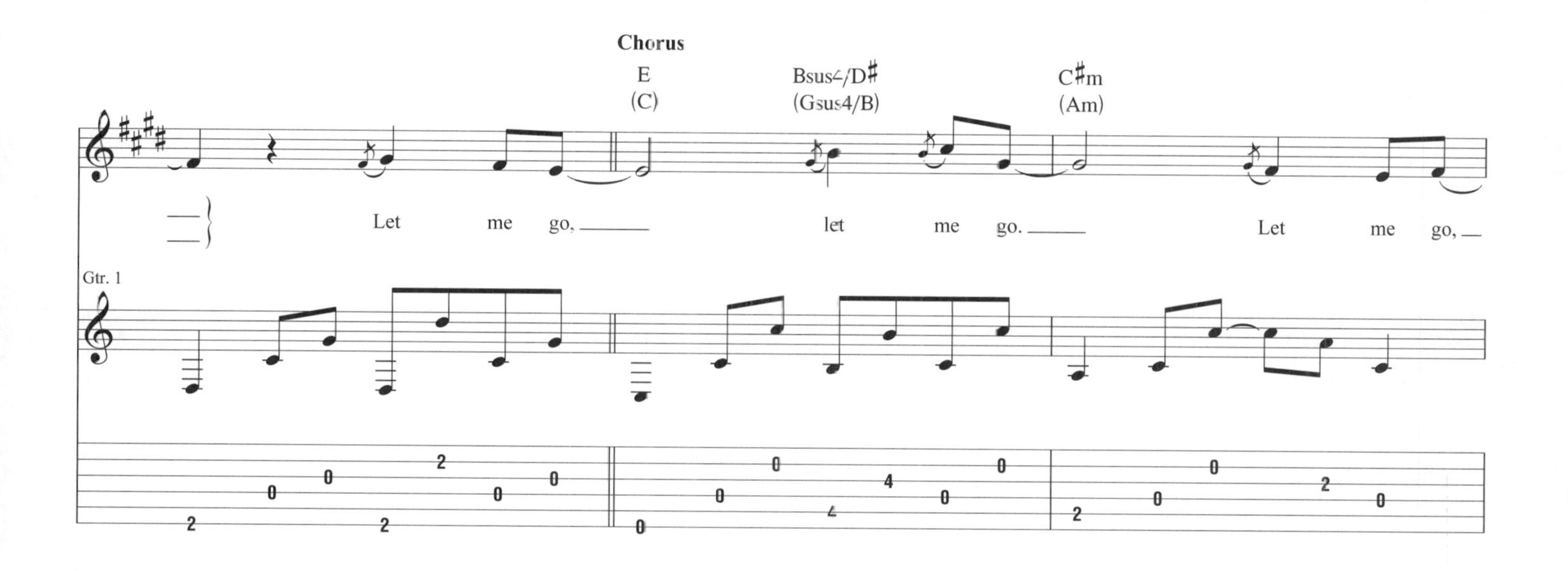
Chorus
E
(C)
Bsus4/D♯
(Gsus4/B)
C♯m
(Am)
Let me go, let me go. Let me go,
Gtr. 1

F♯m7
(Dm7)
A5
(F5)
E
(C)
Bsus4/D♯
(Gsus4/B)
let me go. Let me go, let me go.

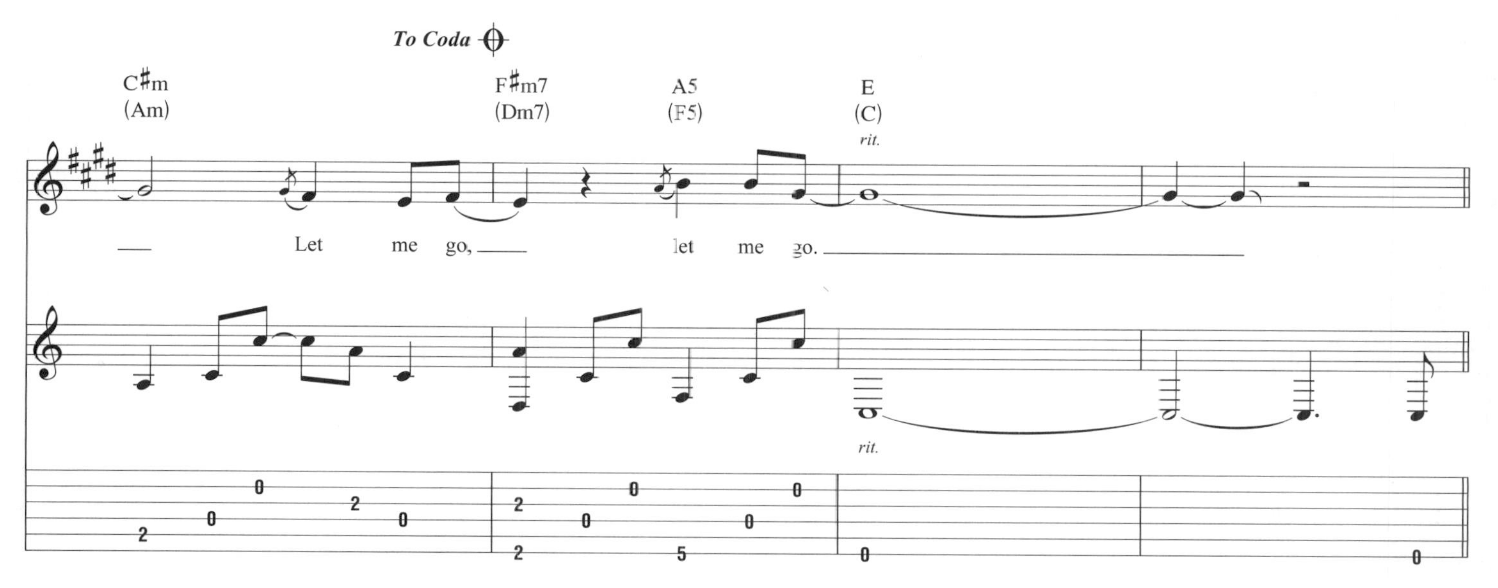
To Coda
C♯m
(Am)
F♯m7
(Dm7)
A5
(F5)
E
(C)
rit.
Let me go, let me go.
rit.

Interlude
Tempo I
E
(C)
E7/D
(C7/B♭)
Amaj9
(Fmaj9)
F♯m7
(Dm7)
A5
(F5)
B5
(G5)
E7
(C7)

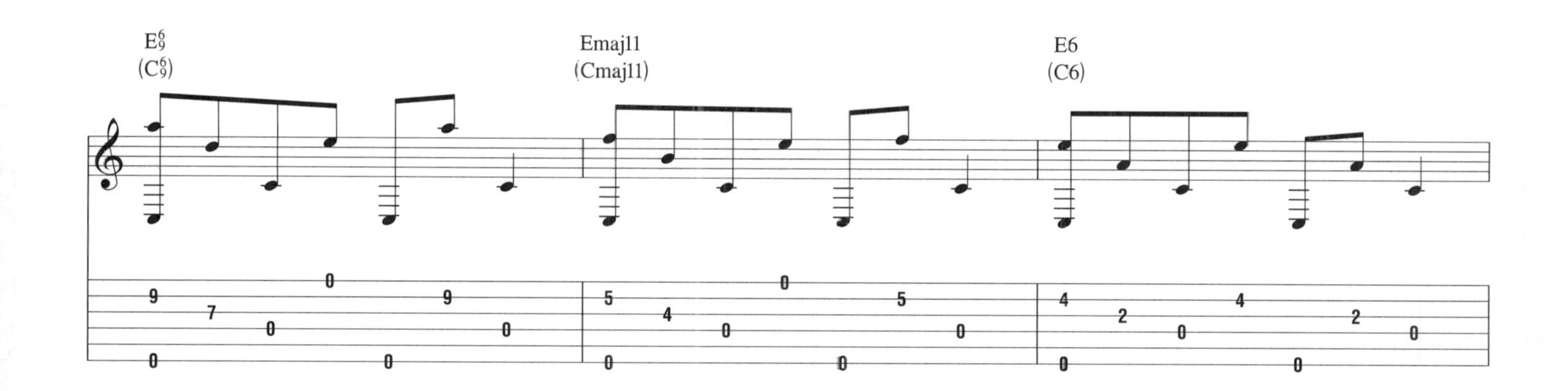
E6/9
(C6/9)
Emaj11
(Cmaj11)
E6
(C6)

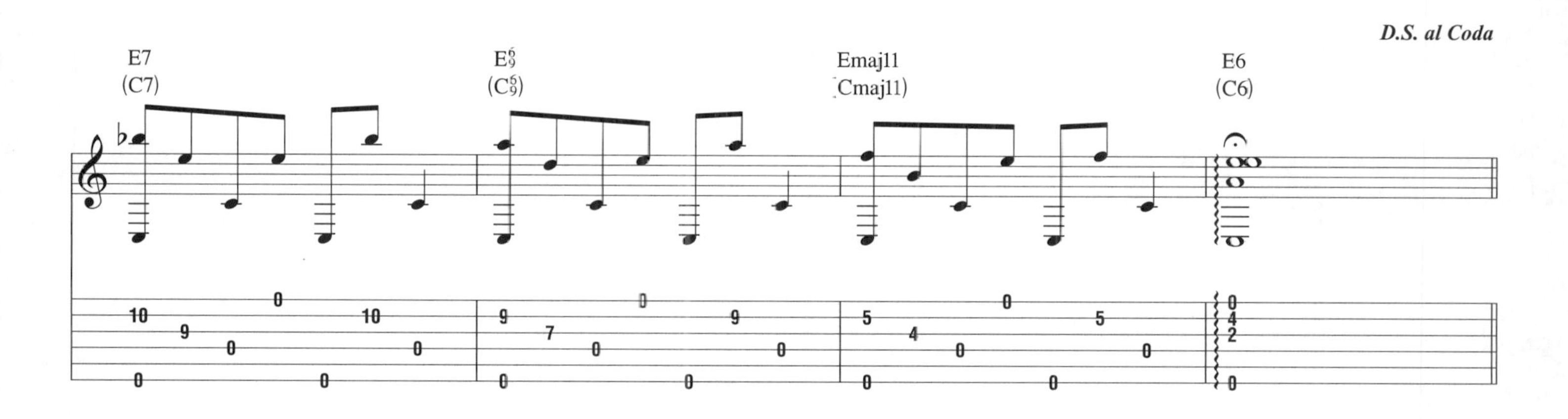
D.S. al Coda
E7
(C7)
E6/9
(C6/9)
Emaj11
(Cmaj11)
E6
(C6)

Coda
F♯m7
(Dm7)
Mm.

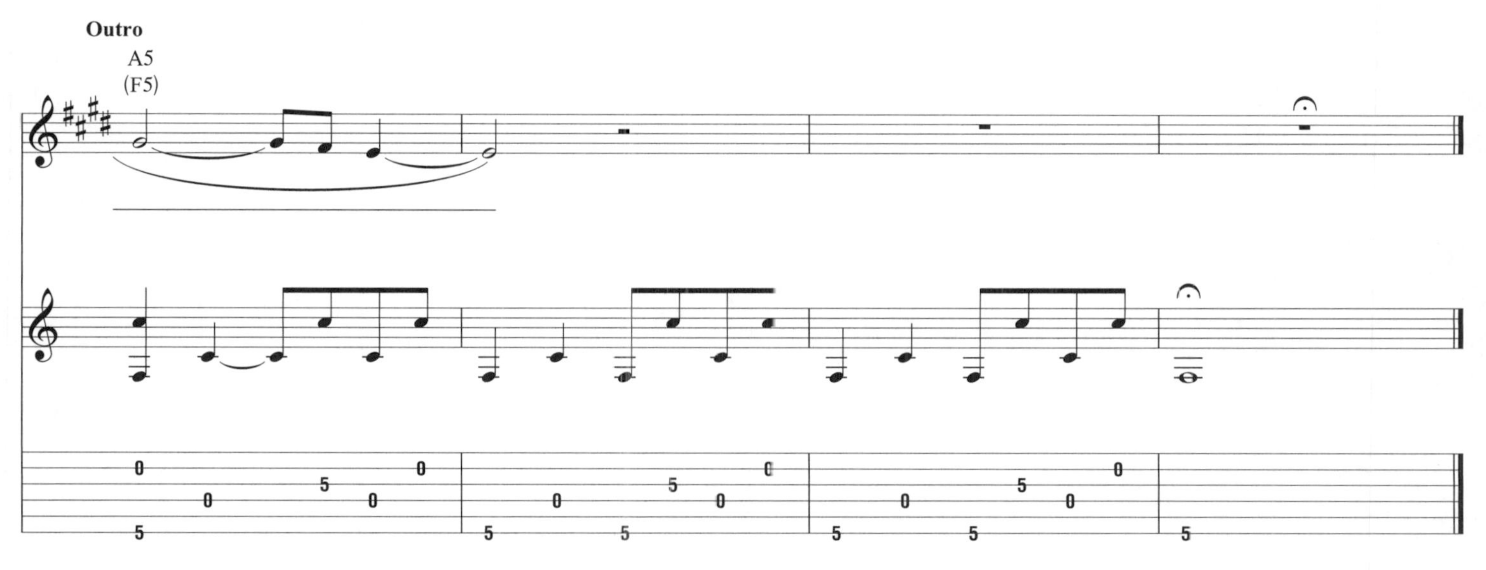
Outro
A5
(F5)

from *Mignonette*

Swept Away
(Sentimental Version)

Words and Music by Scott Avett, Seth Avett and Robert Crawford

Open C tuning, capo VII:
(low to high) C-G-C-G-C-E

*Symbols in parentheses represent chord names respective to capoed guitar. Symbols above represent actual sounding chords. Capoed fret is "0" in tab. Chord symbols reflect basic harmony.

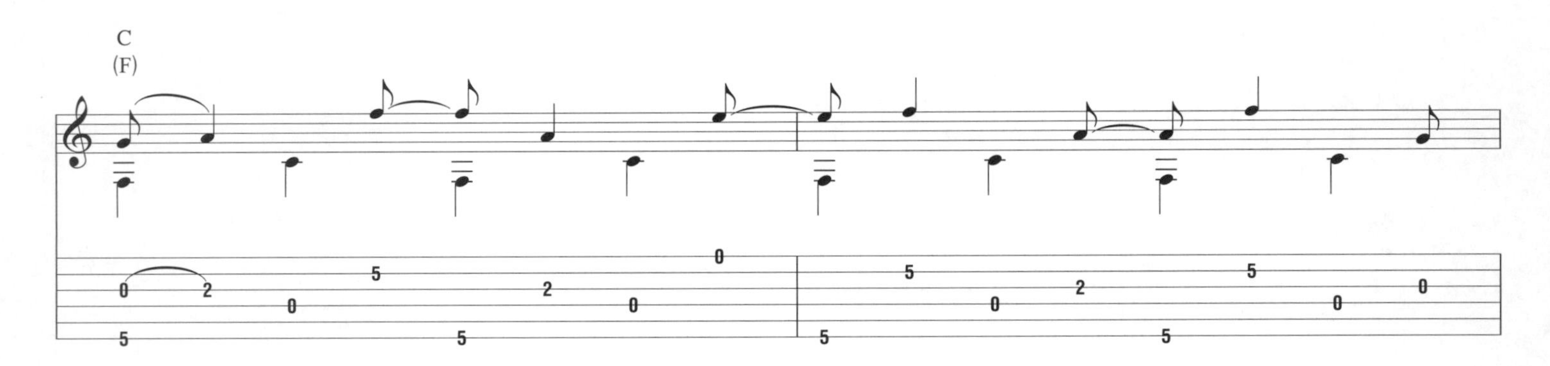

G
(C)
C
(F)
Harm.
G
(C)
D
(G)
Em
(Am)
C
(F)
G
(C)

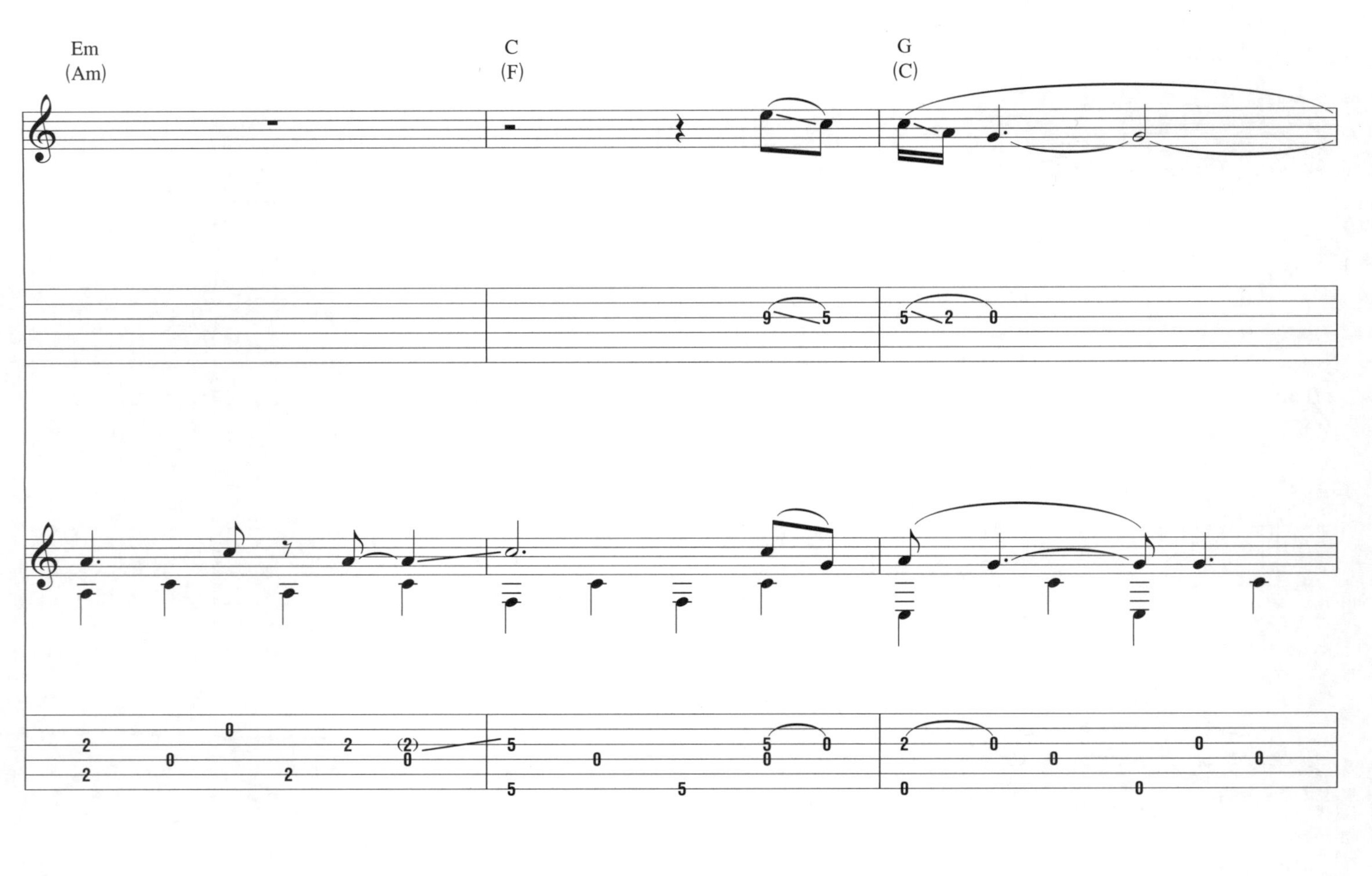
Em
(Am)
C
(F)
G
(C)

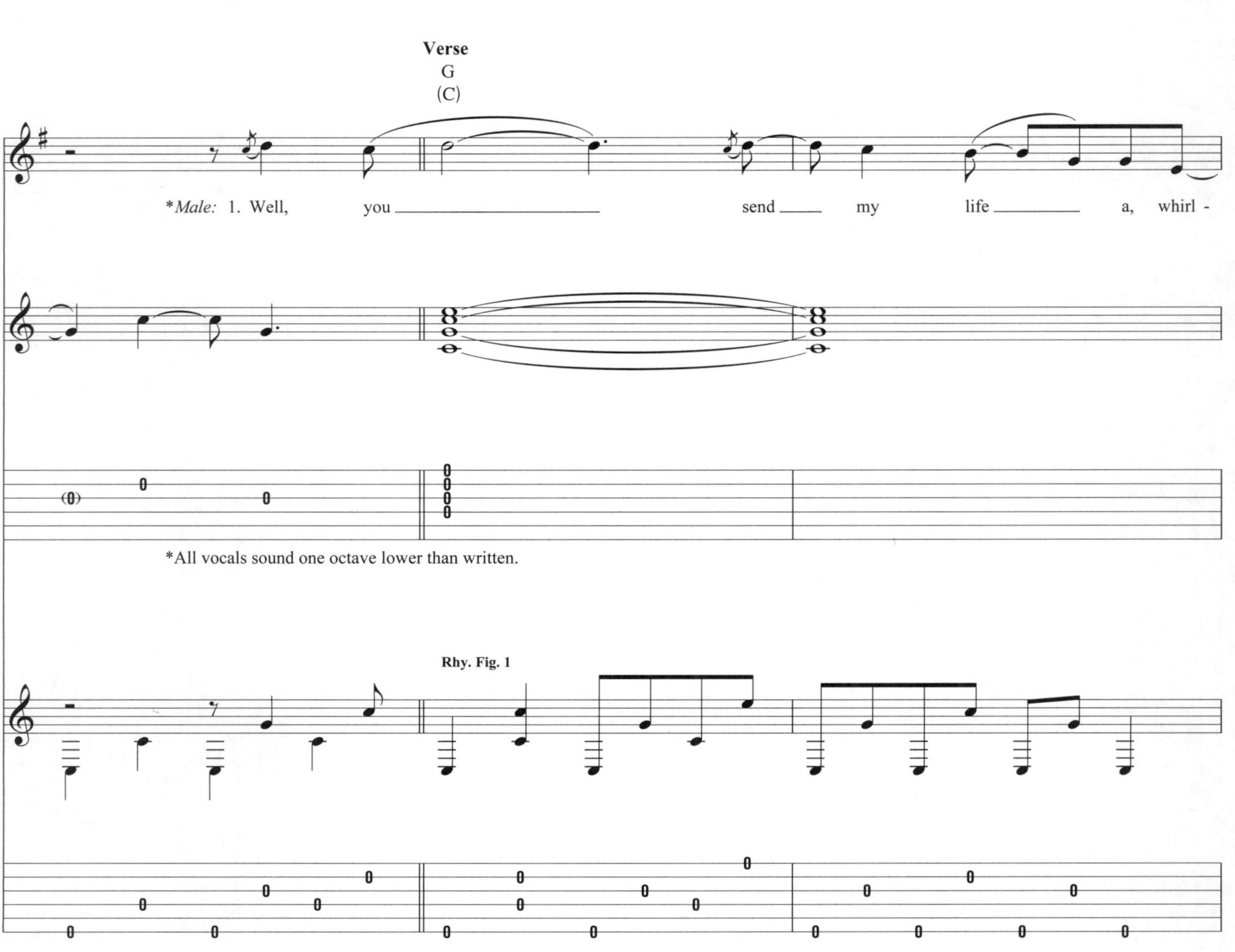
Verse
G
(C)
*Male: 1. Well, you send my life a, whirl -
*All vocals sound one octave lower than written.
Rhy. Fig. 1

C
(F)
G
(C)
- ing, dar - lin', when you're twirl - ing
D
(G)
on the floor. And who
End Rhy. Fig. 1

Gtr. 1: w/ Rhy. Fig. 1
G
(C)
C
(F)
cares about to-mor-row?
What more is to-mor-
Gtr. 2
G
(C)
D
(G)
row than an-oth-er day?
*Male & Female: When you
*Lead voice is male.
Female is high harmony,
male is middle harmony.
Chorus
Em
(Am)
C
(F)
G
(C)
swept me a-way,
yeah, you
Gtr. 2
Gtr. 1
Rhy. Fig. 2
End Rhy. Fig. 2

Em
(Am)
C
(F)
G
(C)
swept me a - way.
Interlude
G
(C)
C
(F)

G
(C)
D
(G)
Male: 2. I see

Verse

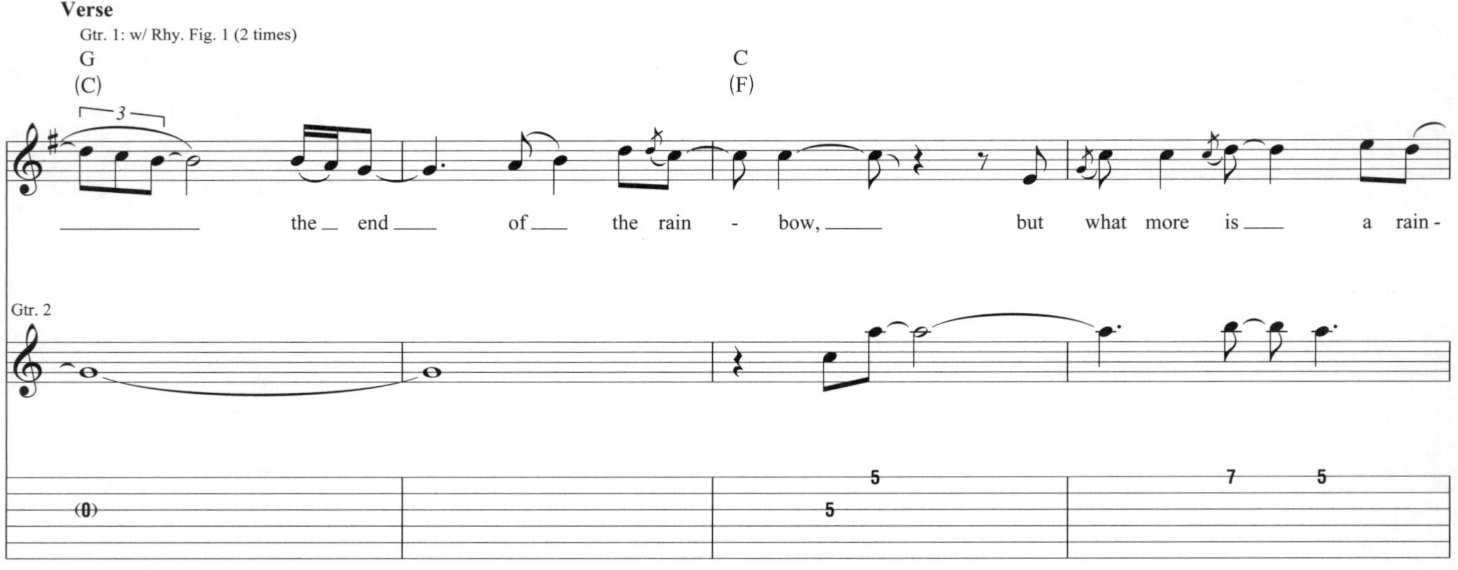
Gtr. 1: w/ Rhy. Fig. 1 (2 times)
G
(C)
C
(F)
the end of the rain - bow, but what more is a rain -
Gtr. 2

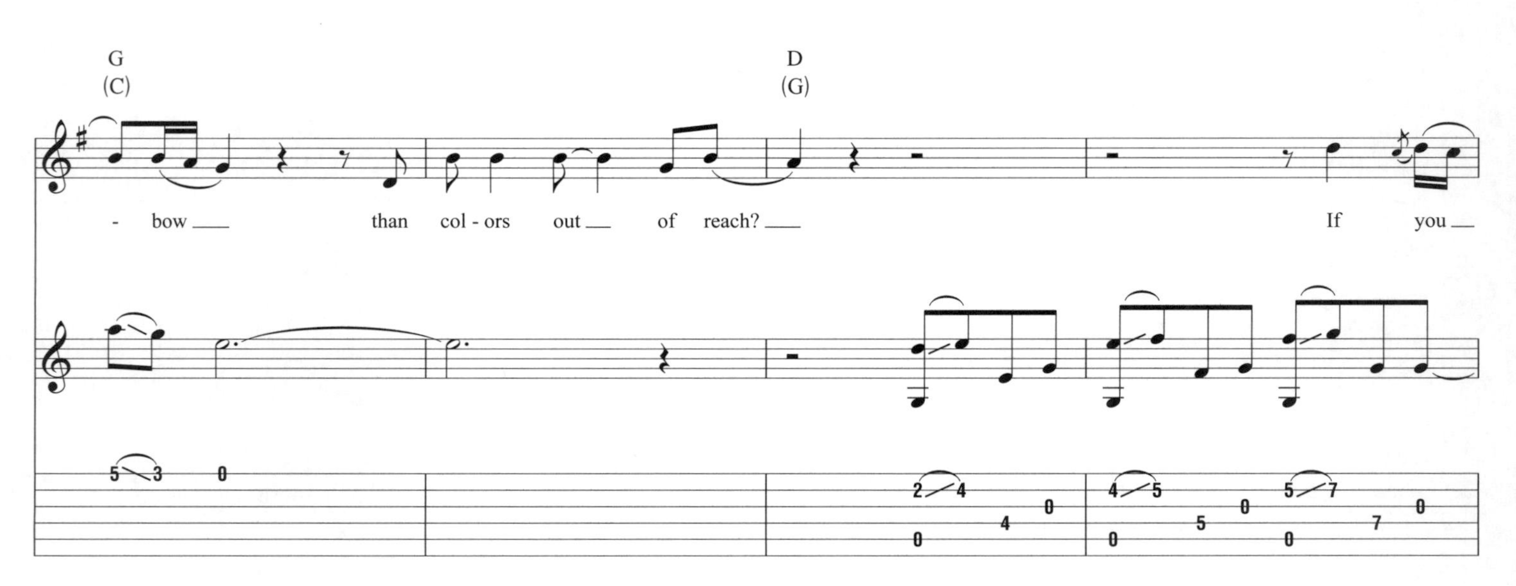
G
(C)
D
(G)
- bow than col - ors out of reach? If you

G
(C)
C
(F)
3
come down to my win - dow and I climb out my win -
G
(C)
D
(G)
- dow, then we'll get out of reach.
*Male & Female: Then you
*Lead voice is male.
Female is high harmony,
other harmonies are male.
Chorus
Gtr. 1: w/ Rhy. Fig. 2 (1 1/2 times)
Em
(Am)
C
(F)
G
(C)
swept me a - way,
Em
(Am)
C
(F)
Yeah, you swept me a - way.

Verse
G
(C)
C
(F)
Male: 3. You said with such honest feel - ing, but what d'you real - ly mean when you
Gtr. 2
Gtr. 1
w/ thumbpick

D
(G)
said that I'm ___ your man? ___
Well, how, _
G
(C)
C
(F)
my dar - lin', can ___ it be ___
you had nev - er seen _

G
(C)
D
(G)
me and you never will again?
*Male & Female: That you
*As before
Chorus
Gtr. 1: w/ Rhy. Fig. 2 (2 times)
Em
(Am)
C
(F)
G
(C)
swept me a-way,
yeah, you
Gtr. 2
Em
(Am)
C
(F)
G
(C)
swept me a-way.

Verse
Gtr. 1: w/ Rhy. Fig. 1 (3 times)
G
(C)
C
(F)
Female: 4. Life is ev - er - chang - ing, but I will al - ways find a con -
G
(C)
D
(G)
- stant and com - fort in your love.
Gtr. 2 tacet
G
(C)
C
(F)
With your heart my soul is bound, and as we dance, I know
G
(C)
D
(G)
that heav - en can be found.
*Male & Female: Well, you
Gtr. 2
*Lead voice is female.

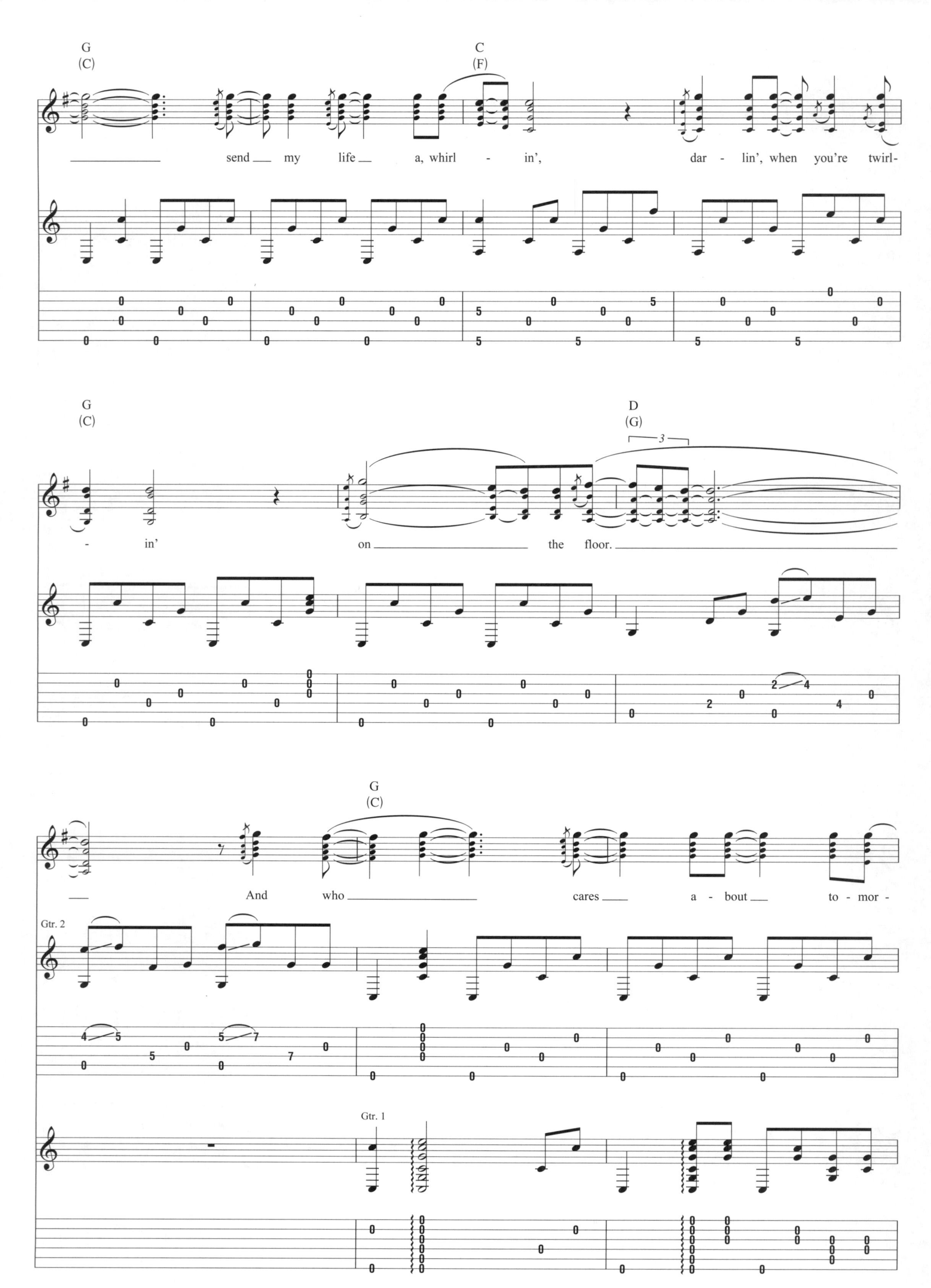
G
(C)
C
(F)
send my life a, whirl - in',
dar - lin', when you're twirl-
G
(C)
D
(G)
3
- in'
on the floor.
G
(C)
And who cares a - bout to - mor -
Gtr. 2
Gtr. 1

C
(F)
G
(C)
- row, what more is to - mor - row than an -
D
(G)
oth - er day? When you
Chorus
Gtr. 1: w/ Rhy. Fig. 2 (2 times)
Em
(Am)
C
(F)
G
(C)
swept me a - way, yeah, you
Gtr. 2

Em
(Am)
C
(F)
G
(C)
swept me a - way,
yeah, you
Outro
Free time
Em
(Am)
C
(F)
rit.
G
(C)
swept me a - way.
rit.
Gtr. 1
rit.
Gtr. 2 tacet
Gtr. 1
Harm.
Pitch: E

from *Emotionalism*

Weight of Lies

Words and Music by Scott Avett, Seth Avett and Robert Crawford

Capo II

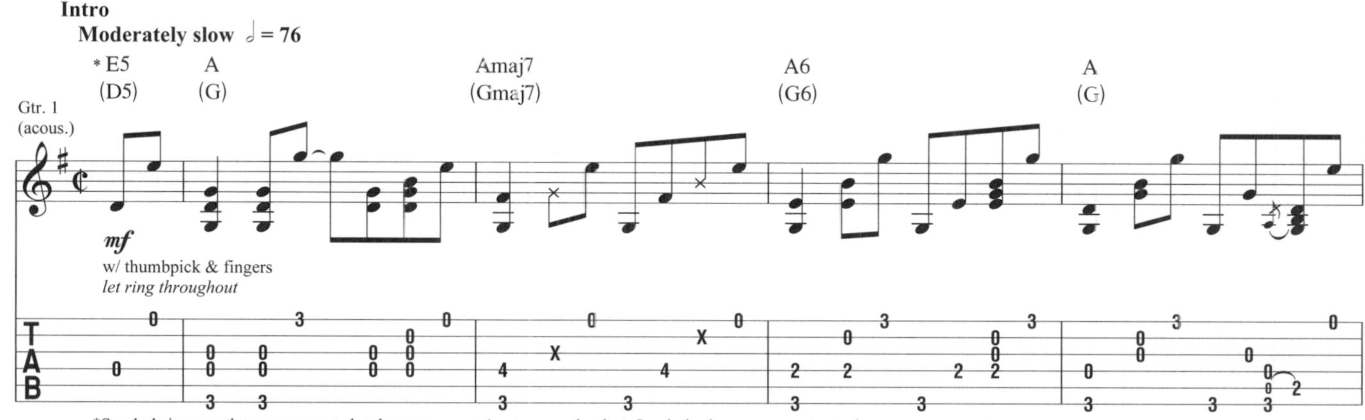

*Symbols in parentheses represent chord names respective to capoed guitar. Symbols above represent actual sounding chords. Capoed fret is "0" in tab. Chord symbols reflect basic harmony

*Composite arrangement

Dmaj7
(Cmaj7)
Dadd9
(Cadd9)
Dmaj7
(Cmaj7)
End Rhy. Fig. 1

Gtrs. 1 & 2: w/ Rhy. Fig. 1 (3 times)
A
(G)
Amaj7
(Gmaj7)
A6
(G6)
Show them all o' your good parts, leave town when the bad

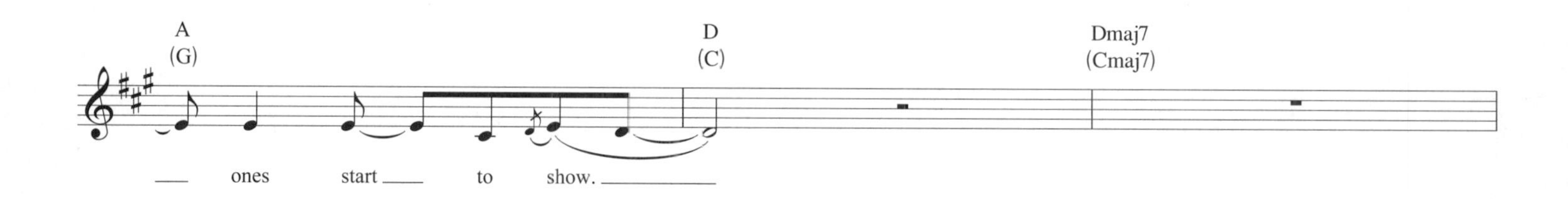
A
(G)
D
(C)
Dmaj7
(Cmaj7)
ones start to show.

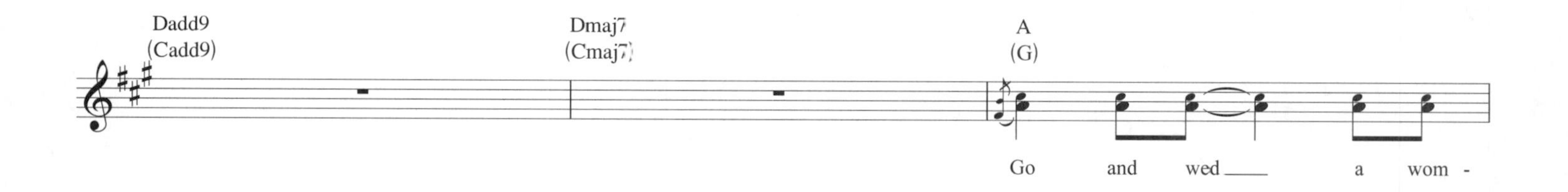
Dadd9
(Cadd9)
Dmaj7
(Cmaj7)
A
(G)
Go and wed a wom -

Amaj7
(Gmaj7)
A6
(G6)
A
(G)
an, a pret - ty girl that you nev - er met.

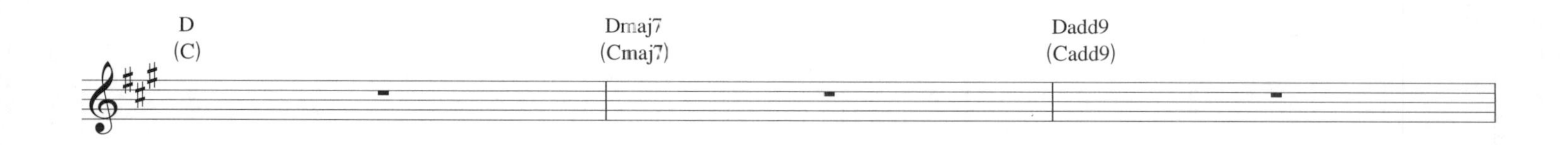
D
(C)
Dmaj7
(Cmaj7)
Dadd9
(Cadd9)

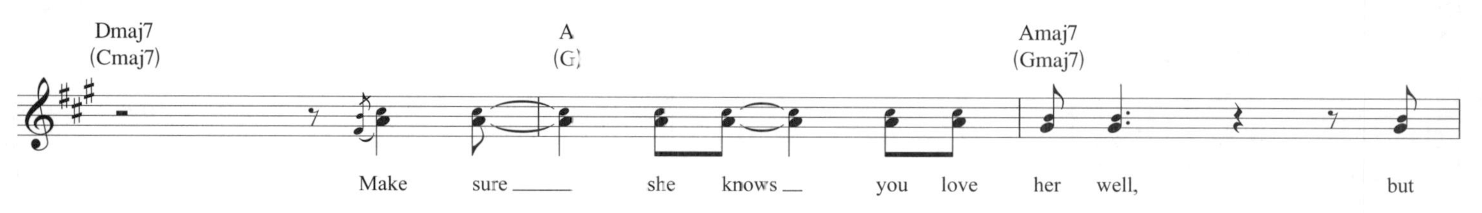
Dmaj7
(Cmaj7)
A
(G)
Amaj7
(Gmaj7)
Make sure she knows you love her well, but

A6
(G6)
A
(G)
D
(C)
don't make an - y oth - er prom - is - es.
Dmaj7
(Cmaj7)
Dadd9
(Cadd9)
Dmaj7
(Cmaj7)
The
Chorus
A
(G)
Bm
(Am)
D
(C)
E7
(D7)
weight of lies will bring you down, and fol-low you to ev - 'ry town. 'Cause
Gtr. 1
Rhy. Fig. 2
w/ thumbpick
Gtr. 2
Rhy. Fig. 3
w/ thumbpick
A
(G)
Bm
(Am)
E7
(D7)
noth - in' hap - pens here that does - n't hap - pen there.
So
End Rhy. Fig. 2
End Rhy. Fig. 3

Gtr. 1: w/ Rhy. Fig. 2
Gtr. 2: w/ Rhy. Fig. 3
A
(G)
Bm
(Am)
D
(C)
when you run, make sure you run to some - thin' and not a -
E7
(D7)
A
(G)
Bm
(Am)
- way from. 'Cause lies don't need an aer - o - plane to
Interlude
Gtr. 1: w/ Rhy. Fig. 1
E7
(D7)
A
(G)
chase you an - y - where. Mm, mm.
Gtr. 2
Rhy. Fig. 4
End Rhy. Fig. 4
w/ thumbpick & fingers
Amaj9
(Gmaj9)
A6
(G6)
A
(G)
D
(C)
Dmaj7
(Cmaj7)
Dadd9
(Cadd9)
Dmaj7
(Cmaj7)

Verse
Gtr. 1: w/ Rhy. Fig. 1 (4 times)
A (G)
Amaj7 (Gmaj7)
A6 (G6)
2. I once heard the worst thing a man can do is draw
A (G)
D (C)
Dmaj7 (Cmaj7)
a hun - gry crowd,
Dadd9 (Cadd9)
Dmaj7 (Cmaj7)
A (G)
tell ev - 'ry - one his name
Amaj7 (Gmaj7)
A6 (G6)
A (G)
in pride and con - fi - dence, but leav - ing out his doubt.

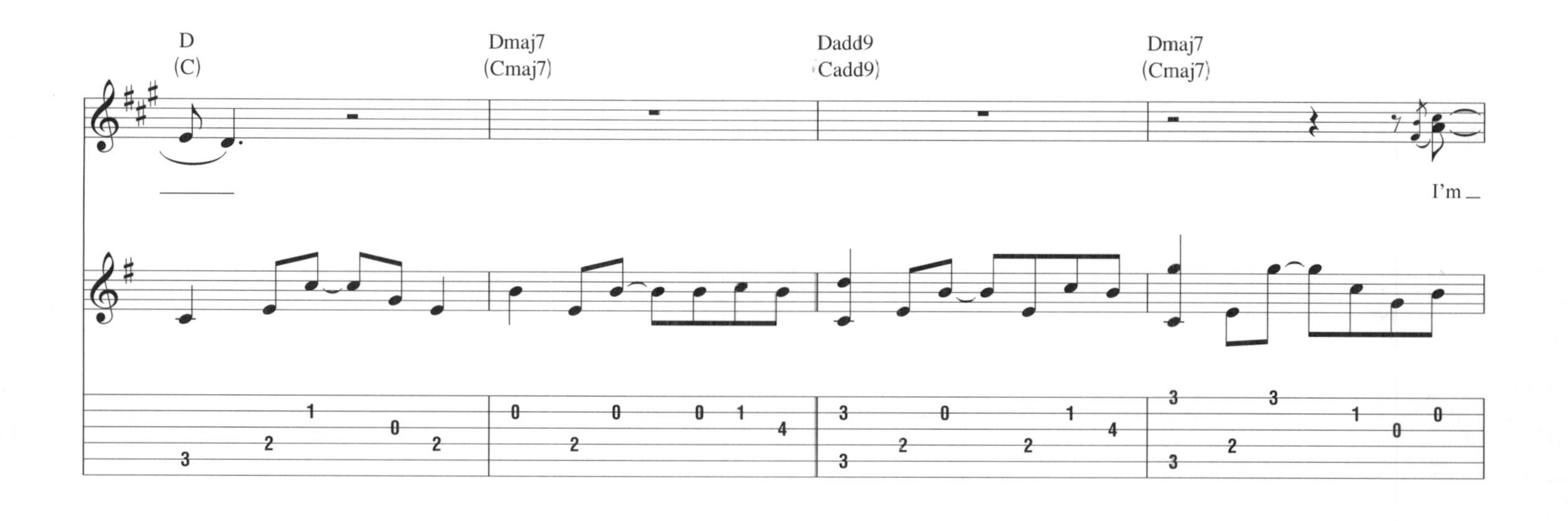
D
(C)
Dmaj7
(Cmaj7)
Dadd9
(Cadd9)
Dmaj7
(Cmaj7)
I'm

Gtr. 2: w/ Rhy. Fig. 1 (2 times)
A
(G)
Amaj7
(Gmaj7)
A6
(G6)
not sure I bought these words, when I was young I knew

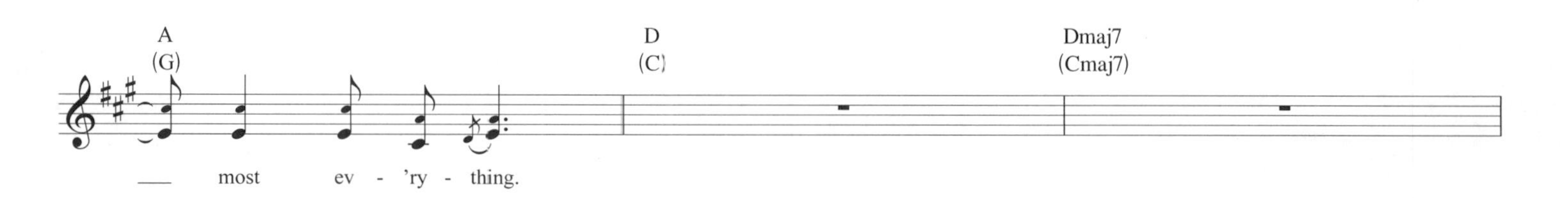
A
(G)
D
(C)
Dmaj7
(Cmaj7)
most ev - 'ry - thing.

Dadd9
(Cadd9)
Dmaj7
(Cmaj7)
A
(G)
These words have nev - er meant

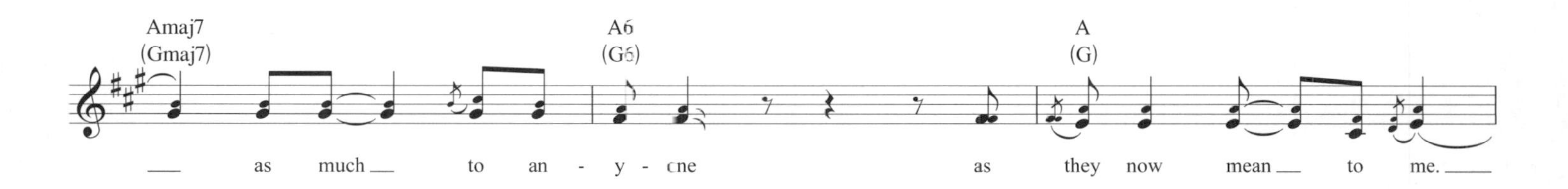
Amaj7
(Gmaj7)
A6
(G6)
A
(G)
as much to an - y - one as they now mean to me.

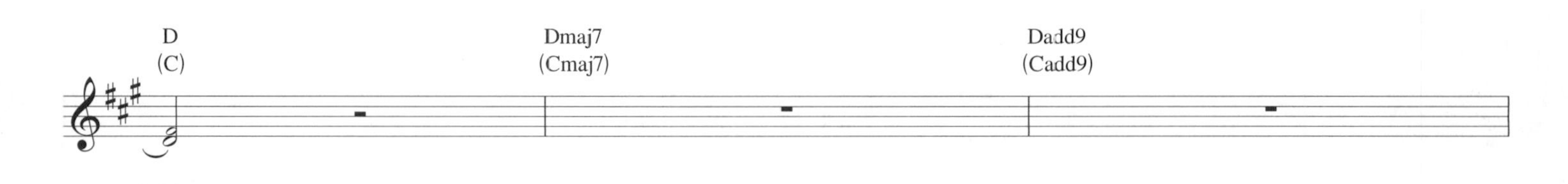
D
(C)
Dmaj7
(Cmaj7)
Dadd9
(Cadd9)

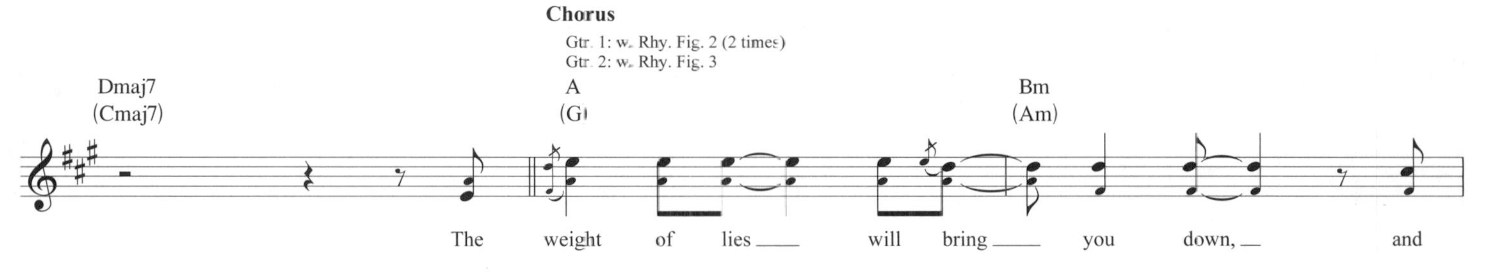
Chorus
Gtr. 1: w/ Rhy. Fig. 2 (2 times)
Gtr. 2: w/ Rhy. Fig. 3
Dmaj7
(Cmaj7)
A
(G)
Bm
(Am)
The weight of lies will bring you down, and

D (C)
E7 (D7)
A (G)
fol - low you to ev - 'ry town. 'Cause noth - in' hap - pens here

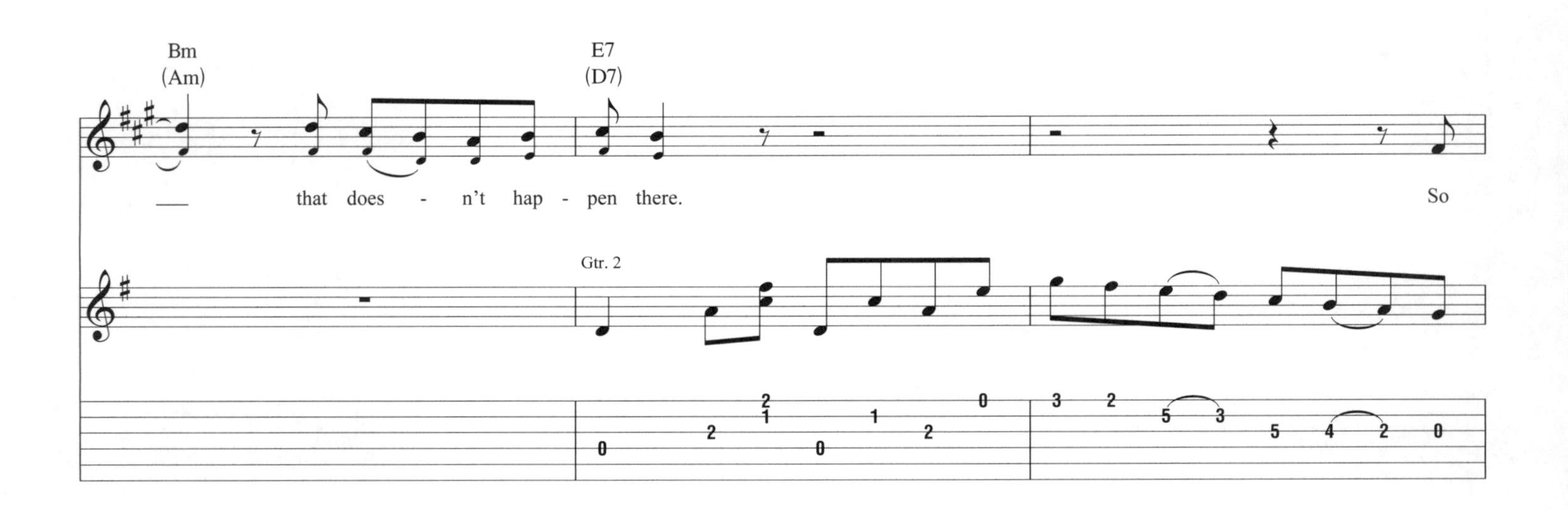
Bm (Am)
E7 (D7)
that does - n't hap - pen there. So
Gtr. 2

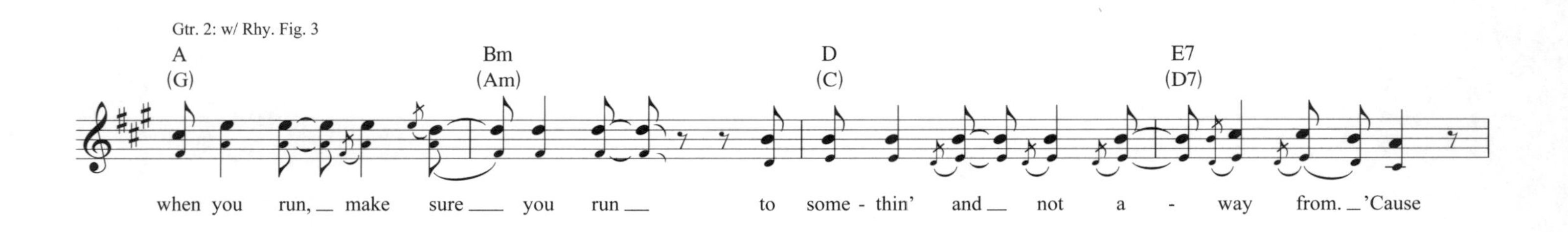
Gtr. 2: w/ Rhy. Fig. 3
A (G)
Bm (Am)
D (C)
E7 (D7)
when you run, make sure you run to some - thin' and not a - way from. 'Cause

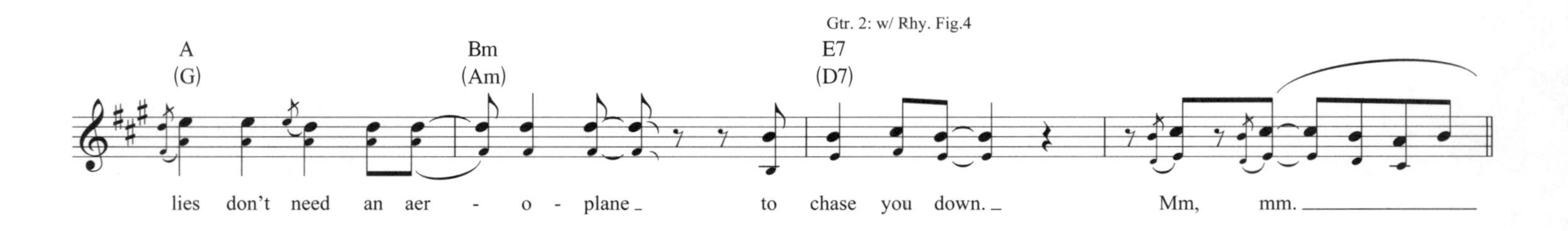
Gtr. 2: w/ Rhy. Fig.4
A (G)
Bm (Am)
E7 (D7)
lies don't need an aer - o - plane to chase you down. Mm, mm.

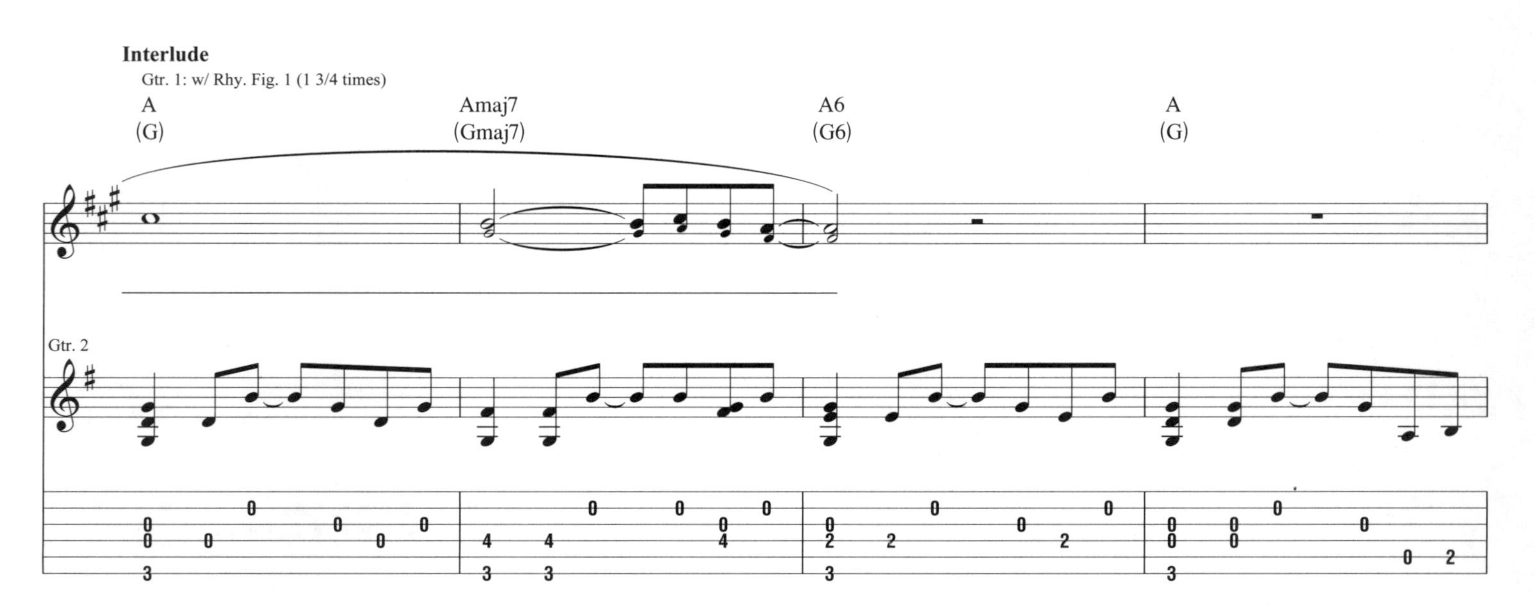
Interlude
Gtr. 1: w/ Rhy. Fig. 1 (1 3/4 times)
A (G)
Amaj7 (Gmaj7)
A6 (G6)
A (G)
Gtr. 2

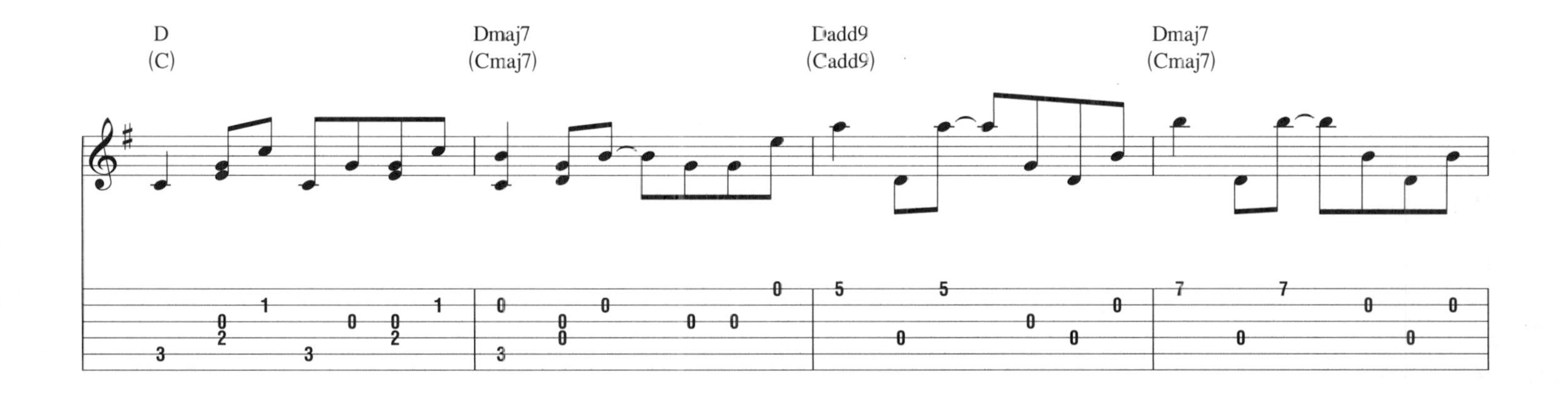
D
(C)
Dmaj7
(Cmaj7)
Dadd9
(Cadd9)
Dmaj7
(Cmaj7)

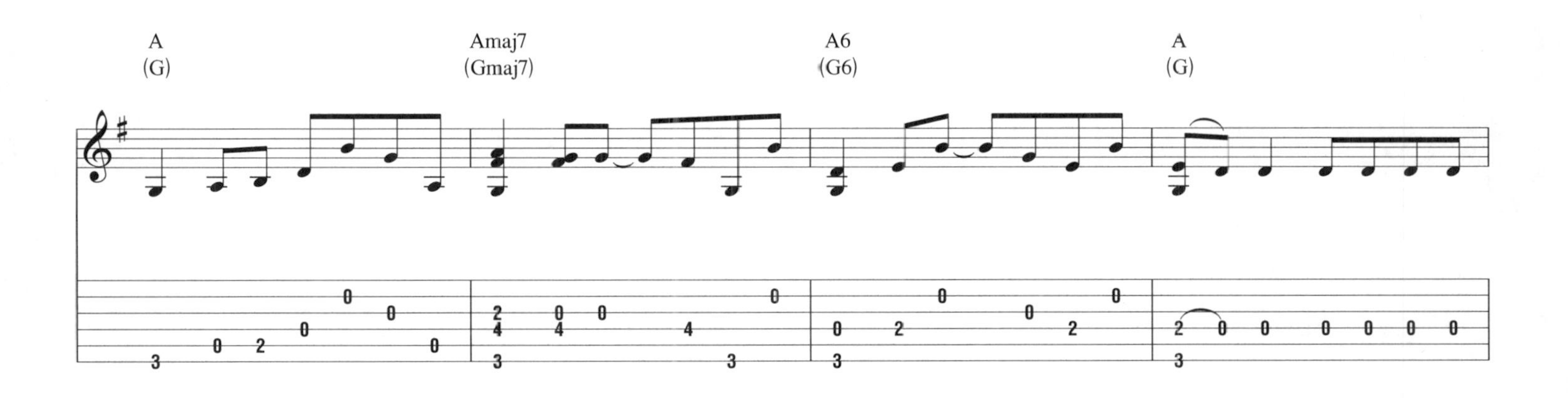
A
(G)
Amaj7
(Gmaj7)
A6
(G6)
A
(G)

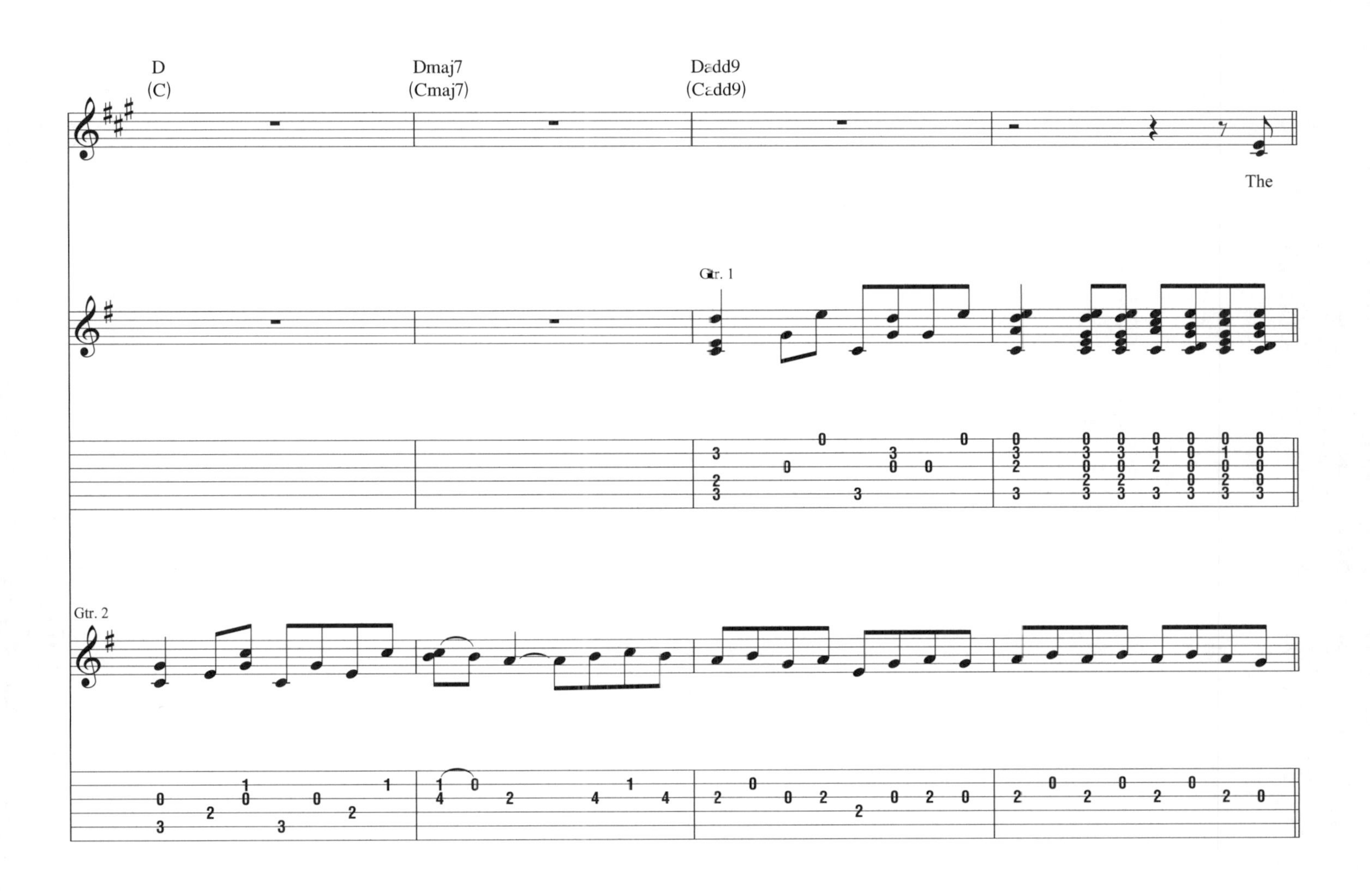
D
(C)
Dmaj7
(Cmaj7)
Dadd9
(Cadd9)
The
Gtr. 1
Gtr. 2

Outro-Chorus
Gtr. 1: w/ Rhy. Fig. 2 (4 times)
Gtr. 2: w/ Rhy. Fig. 3
A (G) Bm (Am) D (C)
weight of lies will bring you down, and fol - low you to ev -
(The weight of lies will bring you down.
E7 (D7) A (G) Bm (Am)
- 'ry town. 'Cause noth - in' hap - pens here that does - n't hap -
Noth - ing hap - pens here.
Gtr. 2: w/ Rhy. Fig. 3
E7 (D7) A (G)
pen there. So when you run, make sure
So when you run,
Gtr. 2
Bm (Am) D (C) E7 (D7)
you run to some - thin' and not a - way from. 'Cause
make sure you run to...

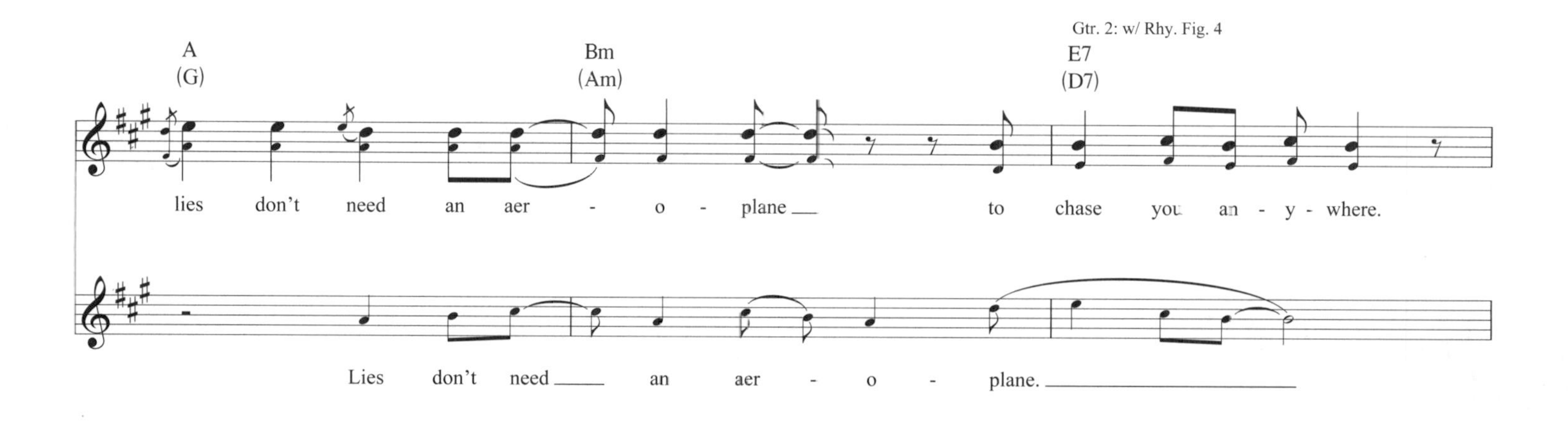
Gtr. 2: w/ Rhy. Fig. 4
A
(G)
Bm
(Am)
E7
(D7)
lies don't need an aer - o - plane to chase you an - y - where.
Lies don't need an aer - o - plane.

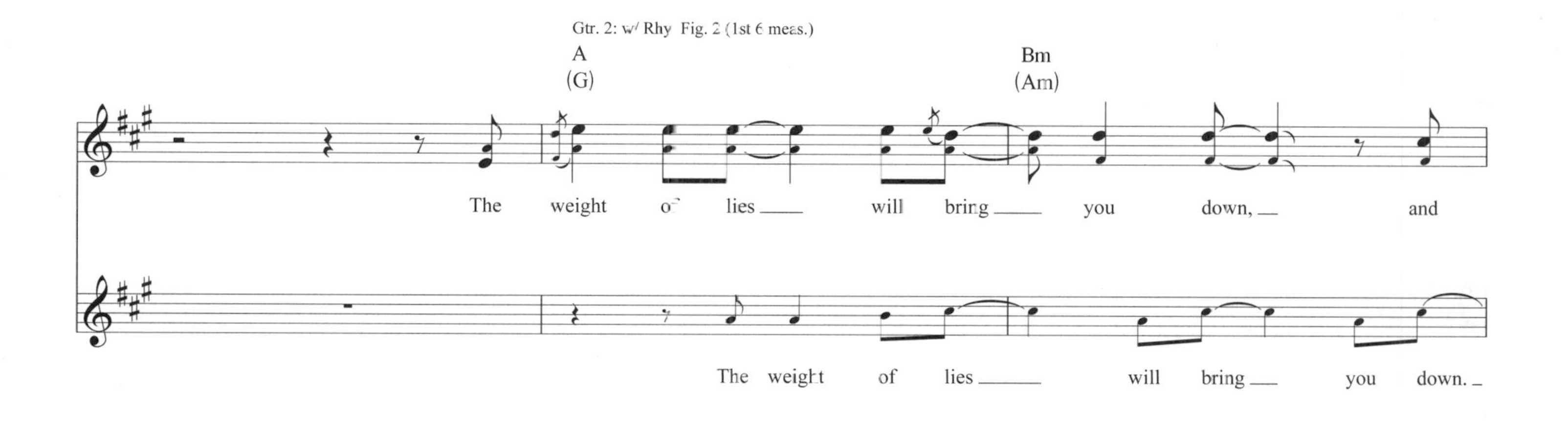
Gtr. 2: w/ Rhy. Fig. 2 (1st 6 meas.)
A
(G)
Bm
(Am)
The weight of lies will bring you down, and
The weight of lies will bring you down.

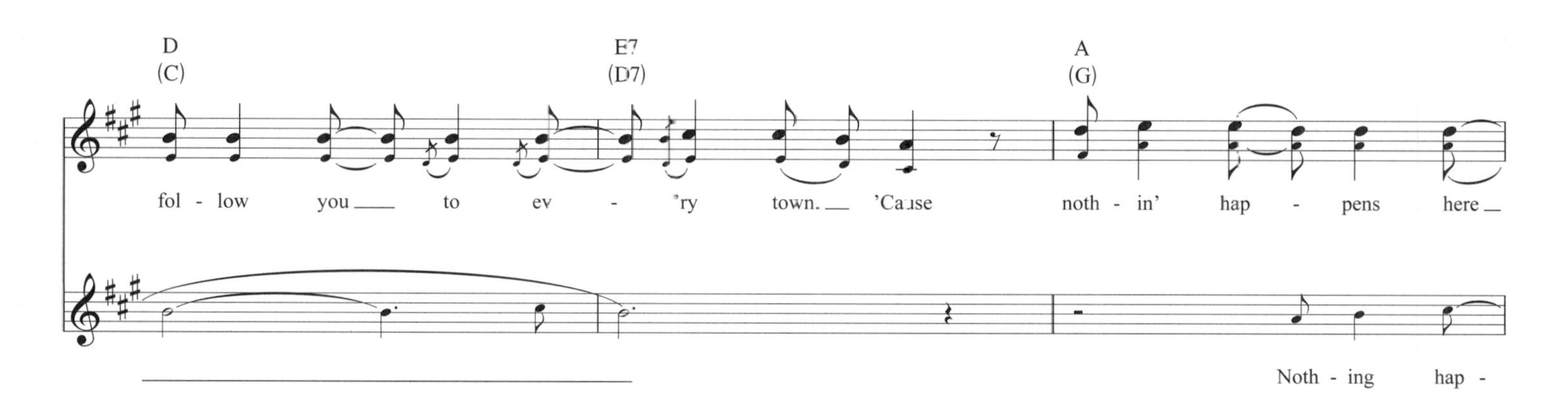
D
(C)
E7
(D7)
A
(G)
fol - low you to ev - 'ry town. 'Cause noth - in' hap - pens here
Noth - ing hap -

Bm
(Am)
E7
(D7)
that does - n't hap - pen there. So
- pens here.
Gtr. 2

Gtr. 2: w/ Rhy. Fig. 3
A
(G)
Bm
(Am)
D
(C)
when you run, make sure you run to some - thin' and not a -
So when you run, make sure you run...

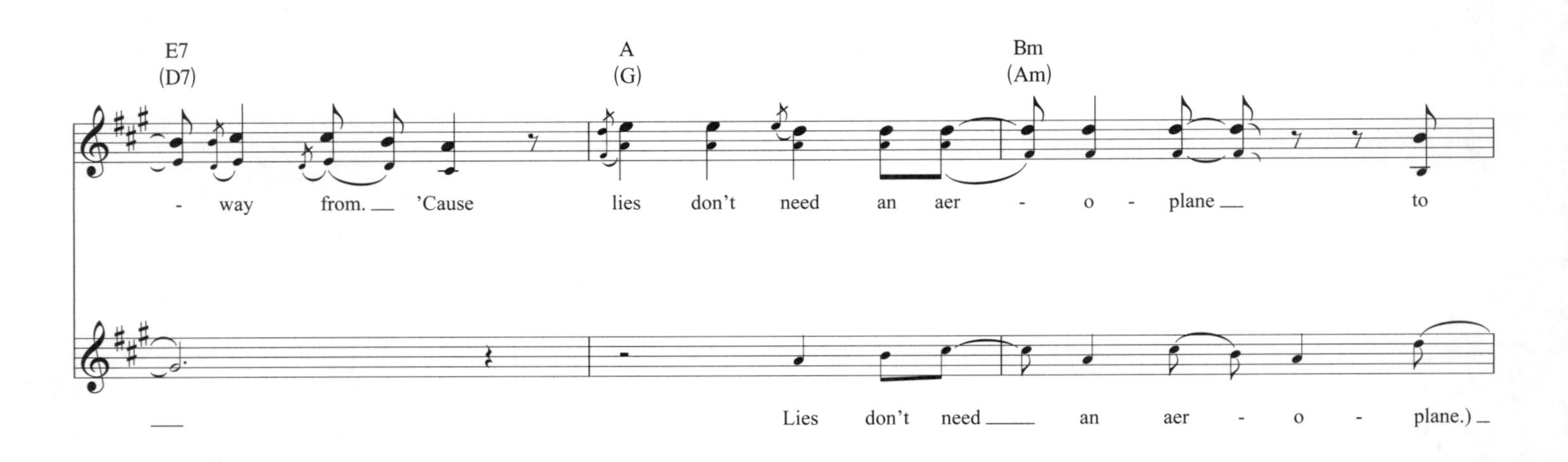
E7
(D7)
A
(G)
Bm
(Am)
- way from. 'Cause lies don't need an aer - o - plane to
Lies don't need an aer - o - plane.)

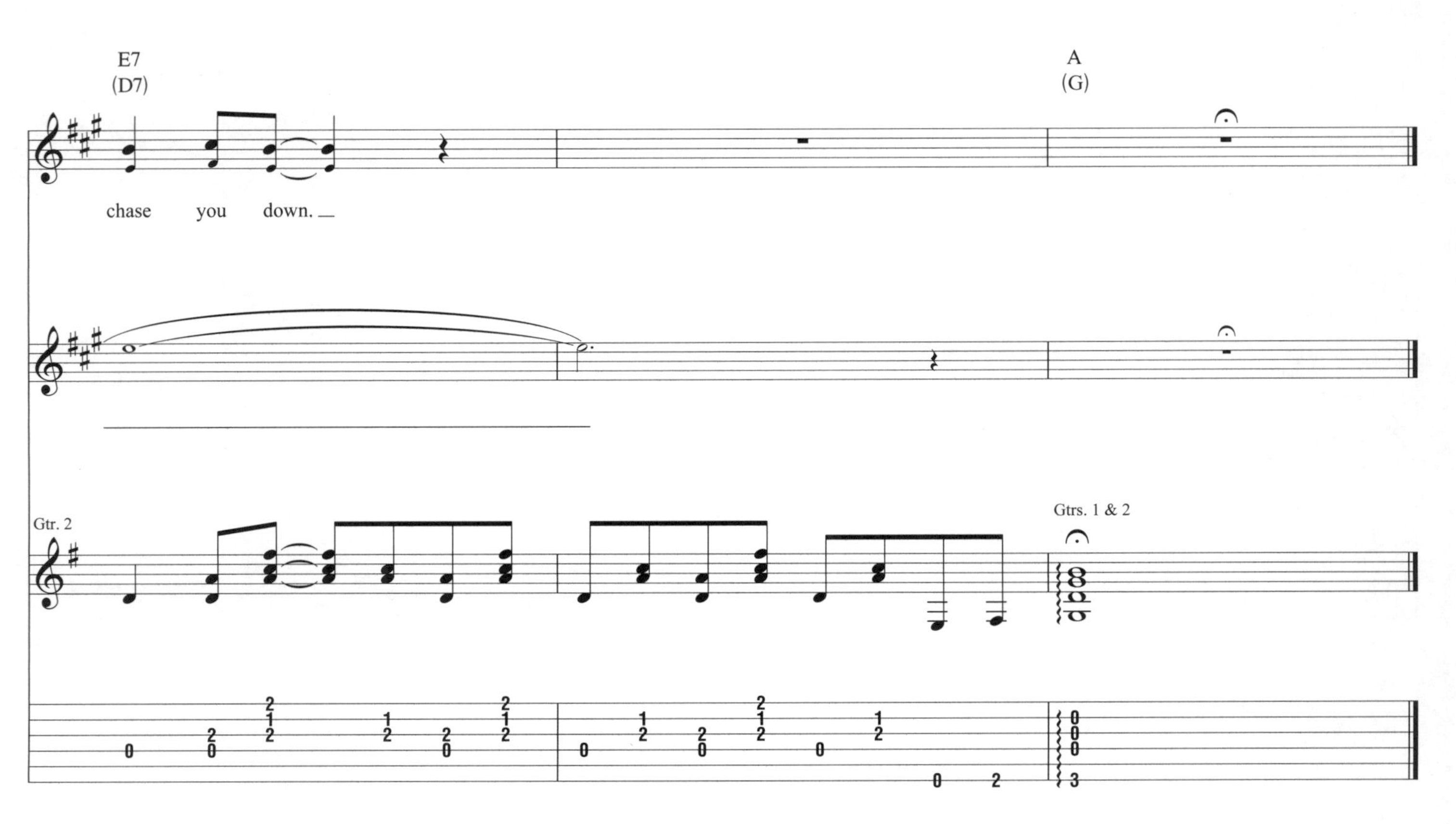
E7
(D7)
A
(G)
chase you down.
Gtr. 2
Gtrs. 1 & 2

GUITAR NOTATION LEGEND

Guitar music can be notated three different ways: on a *musical staff*, in *tablature*, and in *rhythm slashes*.

RHYTHM SLASHES are written above the staff. Strum chords in the rhythm indicated. Use the chord diagrams found at the top of the first page of the transcription for the appropriate chord voicings. Round noteheads indicate single notes.

THE MUSICAL STAFF shows pitches and rhythms and is divided by bar lines into measures. Pitches are named after the first seven letters of the alphabet.

TABLATURE graphically represents the guitar fingerboard. Each horizontal line represents a string, and each number represents a fret.

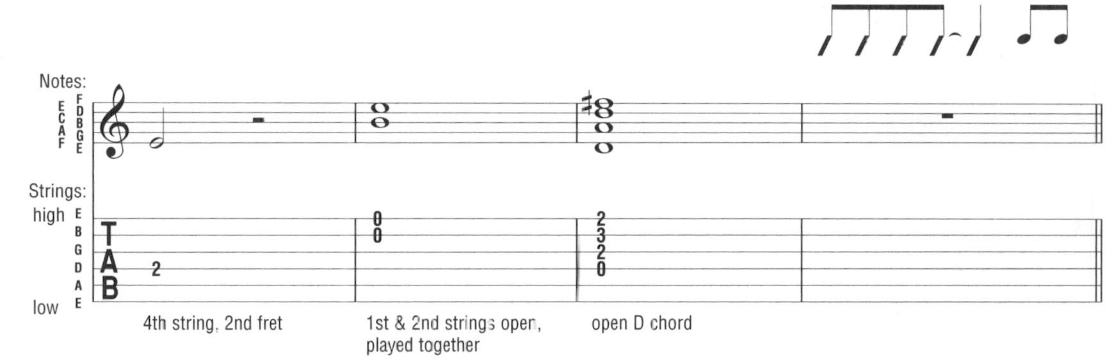

HALF-STEP BEND: Strike the note and bend up 1/2 step.

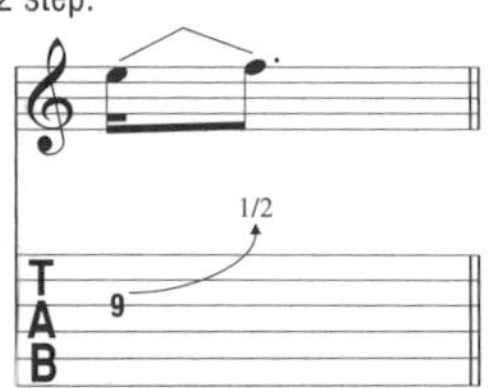

WHOLE-STEP BEND: Strike the note and bend up one step.

GRACE NOTE BEND: Strike the note and immediately bend up as indicated.

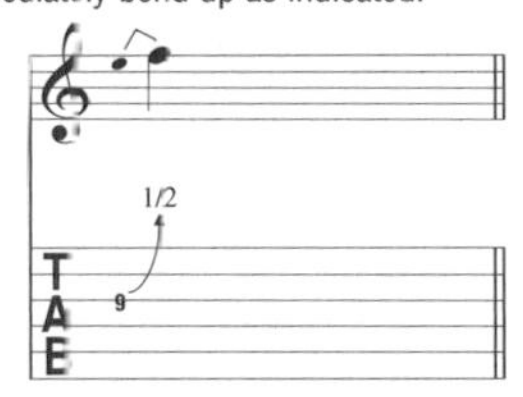

SLIGHT (MICROTONE) BEND: Strike the note and bend up 1/4 step.

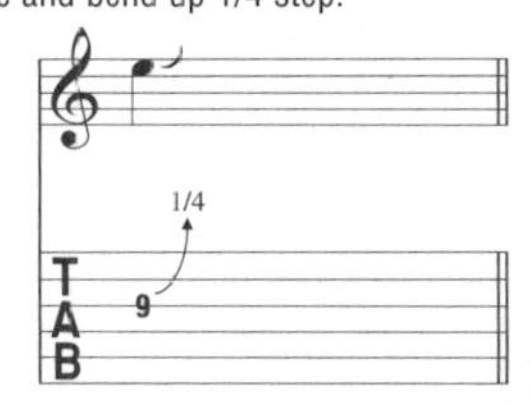

BEND AND RELEASE: Strike the note and bend up as indicated, then release back to the original note. Only the first note is struck.

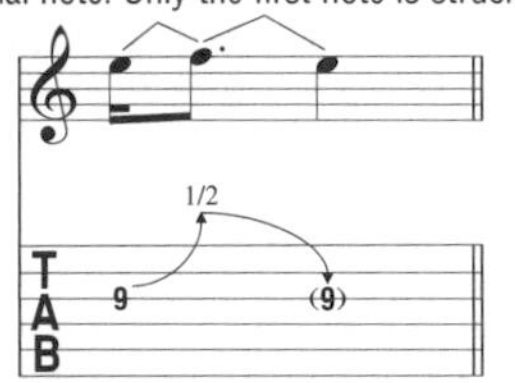

PRE-BEND: Bend the note as indicated, then strike it.

VIBRATO: The string is vibrated by rapidly bending and releasing the note with the fretting hand.

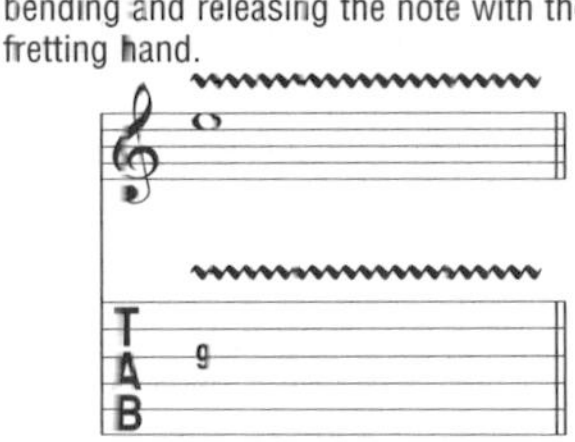

WIDE VIBRATO: The pitch is varied to a greater degree by vibrating with the fretting hand.

HAMMER-ON: Strike the first (lower) note with one finger, then sound the higher note (on the same string) with another finger by fretting it without picking.

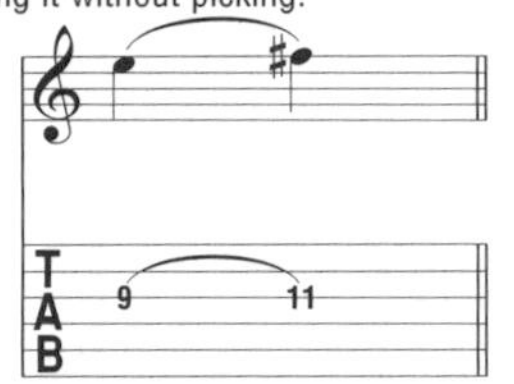

PULL-OFF: Place both fingers on the notes to be sounded. Strike the first note and without picking, pull the finger off to sound the second (lower) note.

LEGATO SLIDE: Strike the first note and then slide the same fret-hand finger up or down to the second note. The second note is not struck.

SHIFT SLIDE: Same as legato slide, except the second note is struck.

TRILL: Very rapidly alternate between the notes indicated by continuously hammering on and pulling off.

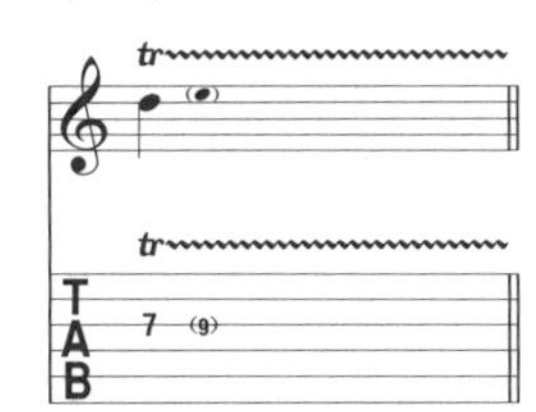

TAPPING: Hammer ("tap") the fret indicated with the pick-hand index or middle finger and pull off to the note fretted by the fret hand.

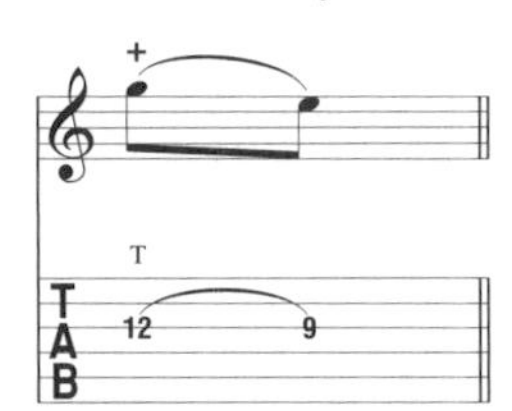

NATURAL HARMONIC: Strike the note while the fret-hand lightly touches the string directly over the fret indicated.

PINCH HARMONIC: The note is fretted normally and a harmonic is produced by adding the edge of the thumb or the tip of the index finger of the pick hand to the normal pick attack.

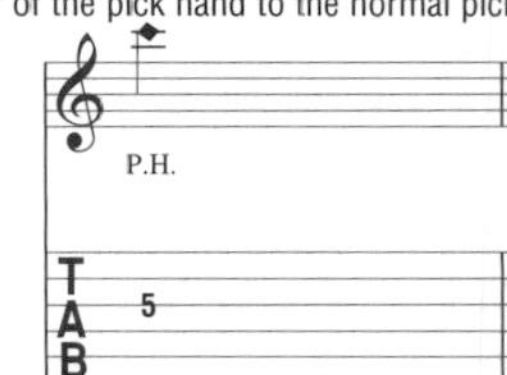

PICK SCRAPE: The edge of the pick is rubbed down (or up) the string, producing a scratchy sound.

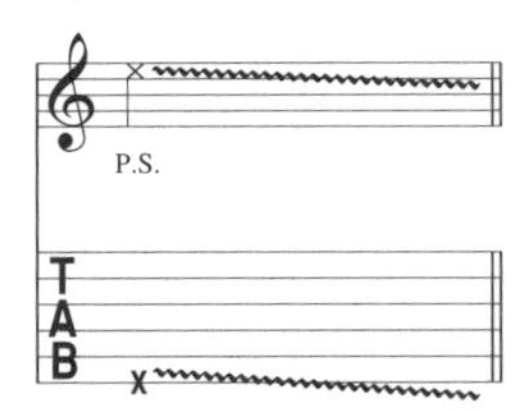

MUFFLED STRINGS: A percussive sound is produced by laying the fret hand across the string(s) without depressing, and striking them with the pick hand.

PALM MUTING: The note is partially muted by the pick hand lightly touching the string(s) just before the bridge.

RAKE: Drag the pick across the strings indicated with a single motion.

TREMOLO PICKING: The note is picked as rapidly and continuously as possible.

VIBRATO BAR DIVE AND RETURN: The pitch of the note or chord is dropped a specified number of steps (in rhythm), then returned to the original pitch.

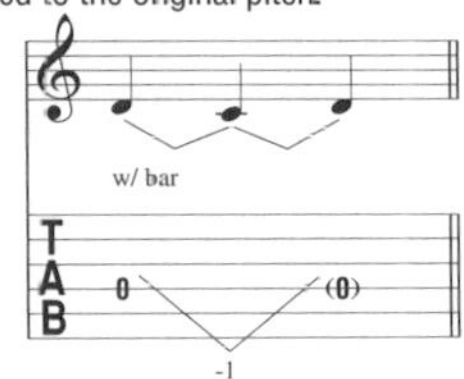

VIBRATO BAR SCOOP: Depress the bar just before striking the note, then quickly release the bar.

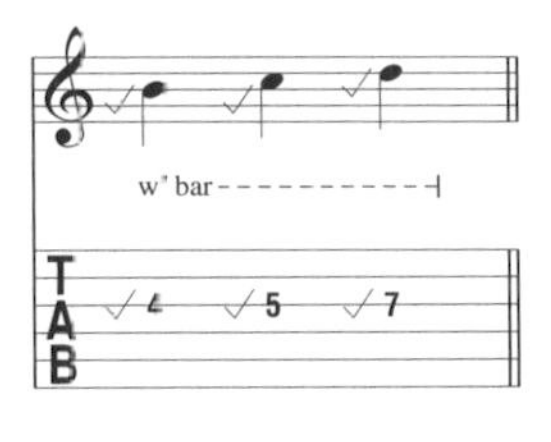

VIBRATO BAR DIP: Strike the note and then immediately drop a specified number of steps, then release back to the original pitch.

RECORDED VERSIONS®

The Best Note-For-Note Transcriptions Available

RECORDED VERSIONS GUITAR®

AUTHENTIC TRANSCRIPTIONS WITH NOTES AND TABLATURE

14037551 AC/DC – Backtracks $32.99
00692015 Aerosmith – Greatest Hits $22.95
00690178 Alice in Chains – Acoustic $19.95
00694865 Alice in Chains – Dirt $19.95
00690812 All American Rejects – Move Along $19.95
00690958 Duane Allman Guitar Anthology $24.99
00694932 Allman Brothers Band – Volume 1 $24.95
00694933 Allman Brothers Band – Volume 2 $24.95
00694934 Allman Brothers Band – Volume 3 $24.95
00123558 Arctic Monkeys – AM $22.99
00690609 Audioslave $19.95
00690820 Avenged Sevenfold – City of Evil $24.95
00691065 Avenged Sevenfold – Waking the Fallen $22.99
00690503 Beach Boys – Very Best of $19.95
00690489 Beatles – 1 $24.99
00694832 Beatles – For Acoustic Guitar $22.99
00691014 Beatles Rock Band $34.99
00694914 Beatles – Rubber Soul $22.99
00694863 Beatles – Sgt. Pepper's Lonely Hearts Club Band $22.99
00110193 Beatles – Tomorrow Never Knows $22.99
00690110 Beatles – White Album (Book 1) $19.95
00691043 Jeff Beck – Wired $19.99
00692385 Chuck Berry $19.95
00690835 Billy Talent $19.95
00690901 Best of Black Sabbath $19.95
14042759 Black Sabbath – 13 $19.99
00690831 blink-182 – Greatest Hits $19.95
00690913 Boston $19.95
00690932 Boston – Don't Look Back $19.99
00690491 David Bowie – Best of $19.95
00690873 Breaking Benjamin – Phobia $19.95
00690451 Jeff Buckley – Collection $24.95
00690957 Bullet for My Valentine – Scream Aim Fire $22.99
00691159 The Cars – Complete Greatest Hits $22.99
00691079 Best of Johnny Cash $22.99
00690590 Eric Clapton – Anthology $29.95
00690415 Clapton Chronicles – Best of Eric Clapton $18.95
00690936 Eric Clapton – Complete Clapton $29.99
00690074 Eric Clapton – The Cream of Clapton $24.95
00694869 Eric Clapton – Unplugged $22.95
00690162 The Clash – Best of $19.95
00101916 Eric Church – Chief $22.99
00690828 Coheed & Cambria – Good Apollo I'm Burning Star, IV, Vol. 1: From Fear Through the Eyes of Madness $19.95
00127184 Best of Robert Cray $19.99
00690819 Creedence Clearwater Revival – Best of $22.95
00690648 The Very Best of Jim Croce $19.95
00690613 Crosby, Stills & Nash – Best of $22.95
00691171 Cry of Love – Brother $22.99
00690967 Death Cab for Cutie – Narrow Stairs $22.99
00690289 Deep Purple – Best of $19.99
00690784 Def Leppard – Best of $19.95
00692240 Bo Diddley $19.99
00122443 Dream Theater $24.99
14041903 Bob Dylan for Guitar Tab $19.99
00691186 Evanescence $22.99
00691181 Five Finger Death Punch – American Capitalist $22.99
00690664 Fleetwood Mac – Best of $19.95
00690870 Flyleaf $19.95
00690808 Foo Fighters – In Your Honor $19.95
00691115 Foo Fighters – Wasting Light $22.99
00690805 Robben Ford – Best of $22.99
00120220 Robben Ford – Guitar Anthology $24.99
00694920 Free – Best of $19.95
00691050 Glee Guitar Collection $19.99
00690943 The Goo Goo Dolls – Greatest Hits Volume 1: The Singles $22.95
00691190 Best of Peter Green $19.99
00113073 Green Day – ¡Uno! $21.99
00116846 Green Day – ¡Dos! $21.99
00118259 Green Day – ¡Tré! $21.99
00701764 Guitar Tab White Pages – Play-Along $39.99
00694854 Buddy Guy – Damn Right, I've Got the Blues $19.95
00690840 Ben Harper – Both Sides of the Gun $19.95
00694798 George Harrison – Anthology $19.95
00690841 Scott Henderson – Blues Guitar Collection $19.95
00692930 Jimi Hendrix – Are You Experienced? $24.95
00692931 Jimi Hendrix – Axis: Bold As Love $22.95
00692932 Jimi Hendrix – Electric Ladyland $24.95
00690017 Jimi Hendrix – Live at Woodstock $24.95
00690602 Jimi Hendrix – Smash Hits $24.99
00119619 Jimi Hendrix – People, Hell and Angels $22.99
00691152 West Coast Seattle Boy: The Jimi Hendrix Anthology $29.99
00691332 Jimi Hendrix – Winterland (Highlights) $22.99
00690793 John Lee Hooker Anthology $24.99
00690692 Billy Idol – Very Best of $19.95
00121961 Imagine Dragons – Night Visions $22.99
00690688 Incubus – A Crow Left of the Murder $19.95
00690790 Iron Maiden Anthology $24.99
00690684 Jethro Tull – Aqualung $19.95
00690814 John5 – Songs for Sanity $19.95
00690751 John5 – Vertigo $19.95
00122439 Jack Johnson – From Here to Now to You $22.99
00690271 Robert Johnson – New Transcriptions $24.95
00699131 Janis Joplin – Best of $19.95
00690427 Judas Priest – Best of $22.99
00120814 Killswitch Engage – Disarm the Descent $22.99
00124869 Albert King with Stevie Ray Vaughan – In Session $22.99
00694903 Kiss – Best of $24.95
00690355 Kiss – Destroyer $16.95
00690834 Lamb of God – Ashes of the Wake $19.95
00690875 Lamb of God – Sacrament $19.95
00690781 Linkin Park – Hybrid Theory $22.95
00690743 Los Lonely Boys $19.95
00114563 The Lumineers $22.99
00690955 Lynyrd Skynyrd – All-Time Greatest Hits $19.99
00694954 Lynyrd Skynyrd – New Best of $19.95
00690754 Marilyn Manson – Lest We Forget $19.95
00694956 Bob Marley– Legend $19.95
00694945 Bob Marley– Songs of Freedom $24.95
00690657 Maroon5 – Songs About Jane $19.95
00120080 Don McLean – Songbook $19.95
00694951 Megadeth – Rust in Peace $22.95
00691185 Megadeth – Th1rt3en $22.99
00690951 Megadeth – United Abominations $22.99
00690505 John Mellencamp – Guitar Collection $19.95
00690646 Pat Metheny – One Quiet Night $19.95
00690558 Pat Metheny – Trio: 99>00 $19.95
00118836 Pat Metheny – Unity Band $22.99
00690040 Steve Miller Band – Young Hearts $19.95
00119338 Ministry Guitar Tab Collection $24.99
00102591 Wes Montgomery Guitar Anthology $24.99
00691070 Mumford & Sons – Sigh No More $22.99
00694883 Nirvana – Nevermind $19.95
00690026 Nirvana – Unplugged in New York $19.95
00690807 The Offspring – Greatest Hits $19.95
00694847 Ozzy Osbourne – Best of $22.95
00690399 Ozzy Osbourne – Ozzman Cometh $22.99
00690933 Best of Brad Paisley $22.95
00690995 Brad Paisley – Play: The Guitar Album $24.99
00694855 Pearl Jam – Ten $22.99
00690439 A Perfect Circle – Mer De Noms $19.95
00690499 Tom Petty – Definitive Guitar Collection $19.95
00121933 Pink Floyd – Acoustic Guitar Collection $22.99
00690428 Pink Floyd – Dark Side of the Moon $19.95
00690789 Poison – Best of $19.95
00694975 Queen – Greatest Hits $24.95
00690670 Queensryche – Very Best of $19.95
00109303 Radiohead Guitar Anthology $24.99
00694910 Rage Against the Machine $19.95
00119834 Rage Against the Machine – Guitar Anthology $22.99
00690055 Red Hot Chili Peppers – Blood Sugar Sex Magik $19.95
00690584 Red Hot Chili Peppers – By the Way $19.95
00691166 Red Hot Chili Peppers – I'm with You $22.99
00690852 Red Hot Chili Peppers –Stadium Arcadium $24.95
00690511 Django Reinhardt – Definitive Collection $19.95
00690779 Relient K – MMHMM $19.95
00690631 Rolling Stones – Guitar Anthology $27.95
00694976 Rolling Stones – Some Girls $22.95
00690264 The Rolling Stones – Tattoo You $19.95
00690685 David Lee Roth – Eat 'Em and Smile $19.95
00690942 David Lee Roth and the Songs of Van Halen $19.95
00690031 Santana's Greatest Hits $19.95
00690566 Scorpions – Best of $22.95
00690604 Bob Seger – Guitar Collection $19.95
00690803 Kenny Wayne Shepherd Band – Best of $19.95
00690968 Shinedown – The Sound of Madness $22.99
00122218 Skillet – Rise $22.99
00691114 Slash – Guitar Anthology $24.99
00690813 Slayer – Guitar Collection $19.95
00120004 Steely Dan – Best of $24.95
00694921 Steppenwolf – Best of $22.95
00690655 Mike Stern – Best of $19.95
00690877 Stone Sour – Come What(ever) May $19.95
00690520 Styx Guitar Collection $19.95
00120081 Sublime $19.95
00120122 Sublime – 40oz. to Freedom $19.95
00690929 Sum 41 – Underclass Hero $19.95
00690767 Switchfoot – The Beautiful Letdown $19.95
00690993 Taylor Swift – Fearless $22.99
00115957 Taylor Swift – Red $21.99
00690531 System of a Down – Toxicity $19.95
00694824 James Taylor – Best of $17.99
00690871 Three Days Grace – One-X $19.95
00123862 Trivium – Vengeance Falls $22.99
00690683 Robin Trower – Bridge of Sighs $19.95
00660137 Steve Vai – Passion & Warfare $24.95
00110385 Steve Vai – The Story of Light $22.99
00690116 Stevie Ray Vaughan – Guitar Collection $24.95
00660058 Stevie Ray Vaughan – Lightnin' Blues 1983-1987 $24.95
00694835 Stevie Ray Vaughan – The Sky Is Crying $22.95
00690015 Stevie Ray Vaughan – Texas Flood $19.95
00690772 Velvet Revolver – Contraband $22.95
00690071 Weezer (The Blue Album) $19.95
00690966 Weezer – (Red Album) $19.99
00691941 The Who – Acoustic Guitar Collection $22.99
00690447 The Who – Best of $24.95
00122303 Yes Guitar Collection $22.99
00690916 The Best of Dwight Yoakam $19.95
00691020 Neil Young – After the Gold Rush $22.99
00691019 Neil Young – Everybody Knows This Is Nowhere $19.99
00691021 Neil Young – Harvest Moon $22.99
00690905 Neil Young – Rust Never Sleeps $19.99
00690623 Frank Zappa – Over-Nite Sensation $22.99
00121684 ZZ Top – Early Classics $24.99
00690589 ZZ Top Guitar Anthology $24.95

Prices and availability subject to change without notice.
Some products may not be available outside the U.S.A.

0714